BUILDING BLOCKS
for Classic Quilts

D1501072

LEISURE ARTS, INC.
Little Rock, Arkansas

EDITORIAL STAFF

Editor-in-Chief: Susan White Sullivan
Designer Relations Director: Debra Nettles
Craft Publications Director: Cheryl Johnson
Special Projects Director: Susan Frantz Wiles
Senior Prepress Director: Mark Hawkins
Art Publications Director: Rhonda Shelby
Technical Writer: Lisa Lancaster
Technical Associates: Frances Huddleston,
Mary Sullivan Hutcheson, and Jean Lewis
Editorial Writer: Susan McManus Johnson
Art Category Manager: Lora Puls
Graphic Designer: Jacob Casleton
Graphic Artist: Francis Huddleston
and Janie Marie Wright
Imaging Technicians: Stephanie Johnson
and Mark R. Potter
Photography Manager: Katherine Laughlin
Contributing Photostylist: Sondra Daniel
Contributing Photographer: Ken West
Publishing Systems Administrator: Becky Riddle
Publishing Systems Assistant: Clint Hanson
Mac IT Specialist: Robert Young

BUSINESS STAFF

Vice President And Chief Operations Officer:
Tom Siebenmorgen
Director Of Finance And Administration:
Laticia Mull Dittrich
Vice President, Sales And Marketing:
Pam Stebbins
Sales Director: Martha Adams
Marketing Director: Margaret Reinold
Creative Services Director: Jeff Curtis
Information Technology Director: Hermine Linz
Controller: Francis Caple
Vice President, Operations: Jim Dittrich
Comptroller, Operations: Rob Thieme
Retail Customer Service Manager: Stan Raynor
Print Production Manager: Fred F. Pruss

Library of Congress Control Number:
2010926119
ISBN-13: 978-1-60900-015-8

table of contents

new york beauty quilt........................... 4

shoofly table topper........................... 12

trip around the world quilt.................... 16

pineapple quilt 22

true lover's knot quilt.......................... 28

hourglasses & geese quilt 34

churn dash maze quilt 38

mariner's compass quilt 44

rail fence quilt 52

building blocks quilt 56

tree of life quilt 62

log cabin wall hanging 68

grandmother's flower garden quilt........ 72

ocean waves quilt.............................. 78

general instructions 85

These vintage and vintage-style quilts are true classics from every corner of quilt-making history.

And they can help you make the best new quilts you'll ever love! That's because all quilts spring from the same desire to make something beautiful and useful. Follow our patterns to recreate these quilts "as is," or remake them to suit your taste. We think you'll agree this collection of table toppers, wall hangings, and bed quilts can be your foundation—your building blocks—for a houseful of quilted treasures. After all, what makes a quilt yours is how you make it—with your choice of fabric and colors, and your individual flair!

new york beauty

When a quilter looks for a block that will broaden her skills and result in a remarkable quilt, the New York Beauty is a frequent choice. The block itself is large and combines triangles with curves. This particular quilt has a pieced sashing between the blocks. A triangle-and-cone border creates a lovely scalloped edge. The earliest New York Beauty quilts date from the mid 1800s, around the time it became fashionable to top a guest's bed with your very best quilt instead of a heavy blanket.

FINISHED BLOCK SIZE:
$15^3/_4$" x $15^3/_4$" (40 cm x 40 cm)

FINISHED QUILT SIZE:
93" x 93" (236 cm x 236 cm)

YARDAGE REQUIREMENTS

Yardage is based on 43"/44" (109 cm/112 cm) wide fabric.

- 10³/₄ yds (9.8 m) of ecru solid fabric
- 8¹/₄ yds (7.5 m) of pink solid fabric
- 3⁷/₈ yds (3.5 m) of green solid fabric
- 8¹/₂ yds (7.8 m) of fabric for backing
- ⁷/₈ yd (80 cm) of fabric for binding
- 101" x 101" (257 cm x 257 cm) square of batting
- Tracing paper

CUTTING THE PIECES

*Follow **Template Cutting** and **Rotary Cutting**, page 85, to cut fabric. Make templates for all patterns on pages 10-11. Cut all strips across the selvage-to-selvage width of the fabric unless otherwise indicated. All measurements include ¹/₄" seam allowances.*

From ecru solid fabric:
- Cut 512 **B's**.
- Cut 16 squares 16¹/₄" x 16¹/₄". From these squares, cut 16 **E's**.
- Cut 944 **F's**.
- Cut 36 **I's**.
- Cut 4 **K's**.
- Cut 148 **N's**.

From pink solid fabric:
- Cut 576 **A's**.
- Cut 64 **D's**.
- Cut 996 **F's**.
- Cut 9 **H's**.
- Cut 156 **O's**.

From green solid fabric:
- Cut 64 **C's**.
- Cut 24 **G's** 2" x 16¹/₄".
- Cut 36 **J's**.
- Cut 2 **L's** – 3" x 80", piecing as needed.
- Cut 2 **M's** – 3" x 85", piecing as needed.

ASSEMBLING THE QUILT TOP

*Follow **Piecing**, page 86, and **Pressing**, page 87, and refer to **Quilt Top Diagram**, page 9, to assemble the quilt top.*

1. For each block, sew 8 **B's** between 9 **A's** to make **Unit 1**. Repeat to make a total of 4 **Unit 1's**.
2. Follow **Sewing Curves**, page 87, and sew 1 **Unit 1** to 1 **C** to make **Unit 2**. Repeat to make a total of 4 **Unit 2's**.
3. Sew 1 **Unit 2** to 1 **D** to make **Unit 3**. Repeat to make a total of 4 **Unit 3's**. Trim outer straight edges of triangles on **Unit 3's** even with edges of **C** and **D**.
4. Sew 4 **Unit 3's** to 1 **E** to complete **Block**.
5. Repeat Steps 1-4 to make 16 **Blocks**.
6. For sashing, sew 14 ecru **F's** between 15 pink **F's** to make **Unit 4**. Repeat to make a total of 48 **Unit 4's**.

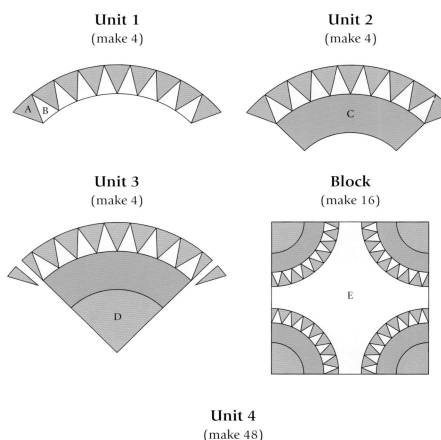

Unit 1
(make 4)

Unit 2
(make 4)

Unit 3
(make 4)

Block
(make 16)

Unit 4
(make 48)

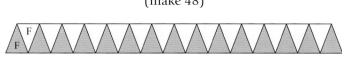

7. Sew 1 **G** between 2 **Unit 4's** to make **Unit 5**. Repeat to make a total of 24 **Unit 5's**. Trim triangles on **Unit 5's** even with edges of **G**.

8. For setting squares, sew 1 **I** between 2 **J's** to make **Unit 6**. Repeat to make a total of 18 **Unit 6's**. Sew 1 **H** between 2 **I's** to make **Unit 7**. Repeat to make a total of 9 **Unit 7's**. Sew 1 **Unit 7** between 2 **Unit 6's** to make **Unit 8**. Repeat to make a total of 9 **Unit 8's**.

9. Sew 3 **Unit 5's** between 4 **Blocks** to make **Row 1**. Repeat to make **Rows 2-4**.

10. Sew 3 **Unit 8's** between 4 **Unit 5's** to make **Unit 9**. Repeat to make a total of 3 **Unit 9's**.

11. Sew 1 **Unit 9** between **Row 1** and **Row 2**. Repeat to add **Rows 3** and **4** and remaining **Unit 9's** to complete **Quilt Top**.

12. For inner pieced border, sew 68 ecru **F's** between 69 pink **F's** beginning and ending with a pink **F**. Repeat to make a total of 4 pieced borders. Square each end of pieced borders by trimming off $1/4"$ outside of point on the beginning and ending **F** triangles.

13. Sew 1 pieced border each to top and bottom of quilt top.

14. Sew 2 **K's** and 1 **L** to 1 remaining pieced border to make **Unit 10**. Repeat to make a total of 2 **Unit 10's**.

15. Matching pieced border to quilt top, sew 1 **Unit 10** to each side of quilt top.

16. Sew 1 **M** each to top and bottom of quilt top.

Unit 5
(make 24)

Unit 6
(make 18)

Unit 7
(make 9)

Unit 8
(make 9)

Row 1

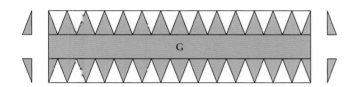

Unit 9
(make 3)

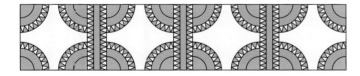

Quilt Top

Unit 10
(make 2)

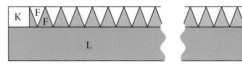

17. For outer pieced borders, sew 37 **N's** between 38 **O's**, beginning and ending with an **O**, to make **Unit 11**. Repeat to make a total of 4 **Unit 11's**.

18. Sew 1 outer pieced border each to top, bottom, and sides of quilt top.

19. Matching right sides, pin 1 O to 1 pieced border. Stitch seam from the outer edge to the dot at the inside point. Pivot the added O to sew the second seam. Pin and sew as before, from inside point to outside dot. Repeat to sew 1 O into each corner of outer pieced border (**Fig. 1**).

Unit 11
(make 4)

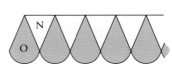

Fig. 1

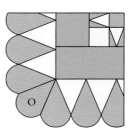

Assembly Diagram

COMPLETING THE QUILT TOP

1. Follow **Quilting**, page 89, to mark, layer, and quilt using **Quilting Diagram**, page 10, as a suggestion. Our quilt is hand quilted.

2. Follow **Making Continuous Bias Strip Binding**, page 93, Steps 1-7, and use a 28" square of binding fabric to make 1¼"w bias binding.

3. Press 1 long edge of bias binding ¼" to wrong side. Press 1 short end of bias binding ½" to wrong side. Matching right sides and raw edges and beginning with pressed end, sew binding to quilt, easing binding around curved edges until binding overlaps beginning end by approximately 2". Trim excess binding. Fold binding over to quilt backing and pin pressed edge in place, covering stitching line. Blindstitch binding to backing.

Quilt Top Diagram

Quilting Diagram

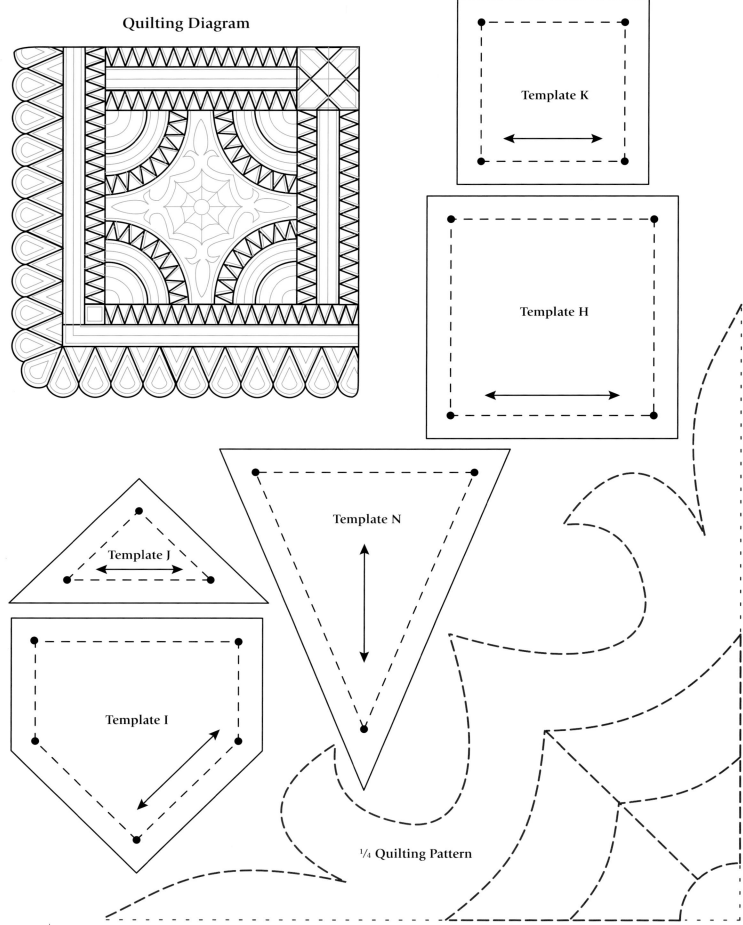

Template K

Template H

Template N

Template J

Template I

¼ Quilting Pattern

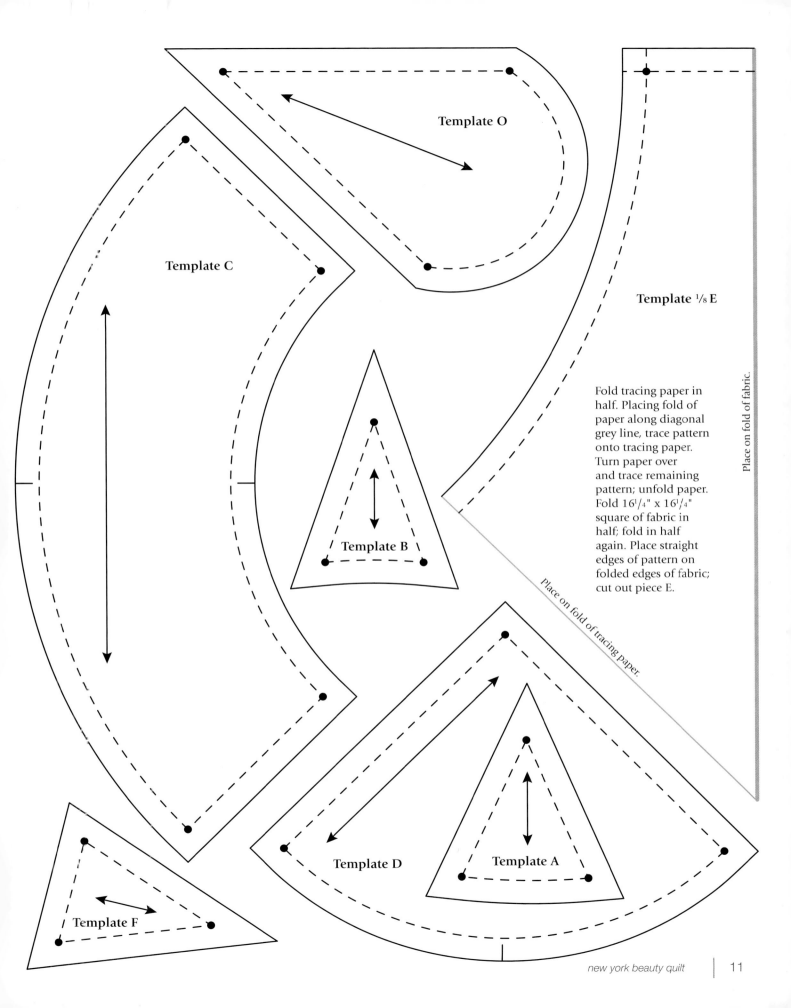

Template O

Template C

Template ⅛ E

Template B

Place on fold of fabric.

Fold tracing paper in half. Placing fold of paper along diagonal grey line, trace pattern onto tracing paper. Turn paper over and trace remaining pattern; unfold paper. Fold 16¼" x 16¼" square of fabric in half; fold in half again. Place straight edges of pattern on folded edges of fabric; cut out piece E.

Place on fold of tracing paper.

Template D

Template A

Template F

shoofly
table topper

The blocks in this delectable
Amish-style quilt may have been
named for an American dessert
that's been served in New England
for more than 200 years. Shoofly
pie is made using just a few simple
ingredients, including molasses.
For that reason, it's easy to imagine
a nineteenth century Amish cook
putting her fresh shoofly pies in a
pie safe to keep the flies away. And
since Amish quilts are usually made
with the same solid-color fabrics
used in Amish clothing, we chose
solids for our table topper.

FINISHED BLOCK SIZE:
4⁷/₈" x 4⁷/₈" (12 cm x 12 cm)

FINISHED TABLE TOPPER SIZE:
35" x 42" (89 cm x 107 cm)

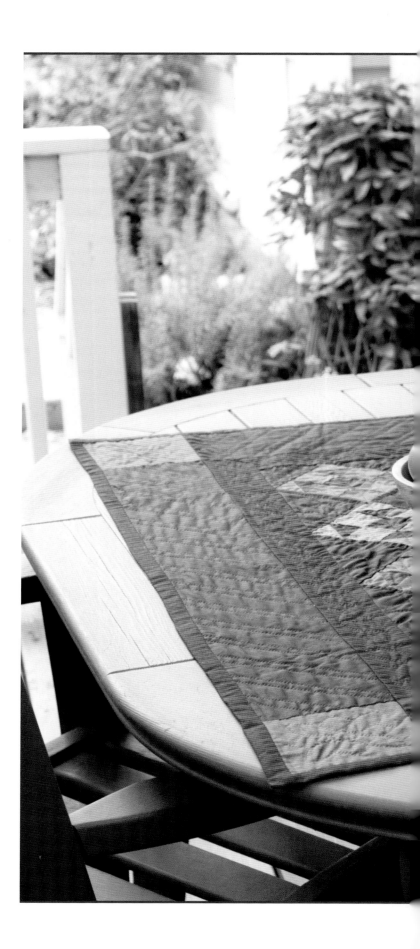

YARDAGE REQUIREMENTS

Yardage is based on 43"/44" (109 cm/112 cm) wide fabric.

- 1¼ yds (1.1 m) of black solid fabric
- ⅜ yd (34 cm) of dark red solid fabric
- ¼ yd (23 cm) of purple solid fabric
- Scraps of assorted medium solids
- Scraps of assorted dark solids
- 2¾ yds (2.5 m) of fabric for backing
- ¾ yd (69 cm) of fabric for binding
- 42" x 49" (107 cm x 124 cm) rectangle of batting

CUTTING THE PIECES

*Follow **Rotary Cutting**, page 85, to cut fabric. Cut all strips across the selvage-to-selvage width of the fabric. Borders include extra length for "insurance" and will be trimmed after assembling quilt top center. All measurements include ¼" seam allowances.*

From black solid fabric:
- Cut 2 **side outer borders** 5" x 36³⁄₈".
- Cut 2 **top/bottom outer borders** 5" x 29½".
- Cut 1 strip 8¼"w. From this strip, cut 3 squares 8¼" x 8¼". Cut squares twice diagonally to make 12 **side triangles**. (You will need 10 and have 2 left over.)
- Cut 1 strip 5³⁄₈"w. From this strip, cut 6 **setting squares** 5³⁄₈" x 5³⁄₈".
- Cut 1 strip 4³⁄₈"w. From this strip, cut 2 squares 4³⁄₈" x 4³⁄₈". Cut squares once diagonally to make 4 **corner triangles**.

From dark red solid fabric:
- Cut 2 **side inner borders** 2⁵⁄₈" x 36³⁄₈".
- Cut 2 **top/bottom inner borders** 2⁵⁄₈" x 25¼".

From purple solid fabric:
- Cut 4 **corner squares** 5" x 5".

From assorted medium solids:
- For **each** of 12 blocks, cut 2 **large squares** 2⁵⁄₈" x 2⁵⁄₈" for triangle-squares and 4 **small squares** 2¹⁄₈" x 2¹⁄₈".

From assorted dark solids:
- For **each** of 12 blocks, cut 2 **large squares** 2⁵⁄₈" x 2⁵⁄₈" for triangle-squares and 1 **small square** 2¹⁄₈" x 2¹⁄₈".

ASSEMBLING THE TOP

*Follow **Piecing**, page 86, and **Pressing**, page 87, to assemble the table topper.*

1. Draw a diagonal line on wrong side of each medium solid **large square**.
2. With right sides together place 1 medium solid large square on top of 1 dark solid **large square**. Stitch seam ¼" from each side of drawn line (**Fig. 1**).
3. Cut along drawn line and press seam allowances to darker fabric to make 2 **Triangle-Squares**. Make 4 **Triangle-Squares**. Trim each Triangle-Square to 2¹⁄₈" x 2¹⁄₈".
4. Sew 2 **triangle-squares** and 1 **small square** together to make **Unit 1**. Make 2 **Unit 1's**.
5. Sew 3 **small squares** together to make 1 **Unit 2**.
6. Sew **Unit 1's** and **Unit 2** together to make **Block**.
7. Repeat Steps 2-6 to make a total of 12 **Blocks**.
8. Referring to **Assembly Diagram**, sew **corner triangles**, **side triangles**, **Blocks**, and **setting squares** together into diagonal rows. Sew rows together to make center section of table topper.
9. Measure width across center of table topper. Trim top and bottom inner borders to determined measurement.
10. Sew **top** and **bottom inner borders** to center.

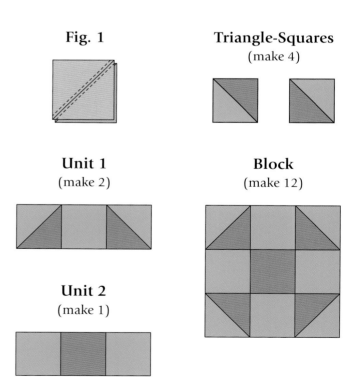

Fig. 1

Triangle-Squares
(make 4)

Unit 1
(make 2)

Block
(make 12)

Unit 2
(make 1)

11. Measure length through center (including added borders). Trim side inner borders to determined measurement.
12. Sew side inner borders to table topper.
13. Measure width across center of table topper. Trim top and bottom outer borders to determined measurement. Measure length through center. Trim side outer borders to determined measurement.

Assembly Diagram

Quilting Diagram

14. Sew **top** and **bottom outer borders** to table topper. Sew 1 **corner square** to each end of **side outer borders**; sew on **borders** to complete **Table Topper**.

COMPLETING THE TABLE TOPPER
1. Follow **Quilting**, page 89, to mark, layer, and quilt using **Quilting Diagram** as a suggestion. Our table topper is hand quilted.
2. Cut a 22" square of binding fabric. Follow **Binding**, page 93, to bind table topper using $2^{1}/_{2}$"w continuous bias binding with overlapped corners.

Table Topper Top Diagram

trip around the world

If you want to make a quilt with plenty of color, consider a design that uses the simplest piecing. The entire Trip Around the World quilt top is considered a one-patch block because it doesn't repeat. Instead, it uses same-size squares arranged in a concentric color pattern.

FINISHED QUILT SIZE:
78³/₄" x 78³/₄" (200 cm x 200 cm)

YARDAGE REQUIREMENTS

Yardage is based on 43"/44" (109 cm/112 cm) wide fabric.

- 2³/₈ yds (2.2 m) of green print fabric for outer borders
- 2¹/₄ yds (2.1 m) of yellow print fabric for middle borders
- 2¹/₈ yds (1.9 m) of red print fabric for inner borders
- ¹/₂ yd (46 cm) **each** of medium yellow, light yellow, navy, dark blue, medium blue, light blue, red, dark pink, medium pink, light pink, olive green, dark green, medium green, light green, orange, and dark yellow print fabrics
- 7¹/₄ yds (6.6 m) of fabric for backing
- 1 yd (91 cm) of fabric for binding
- 86" x 86" (218 cm x 218 cm) square of batting

CUTTING THE PIECES

*Follow **Rotary Cutting**, page 85, to cut fabric. Cut all strips across the selvage-to-selvage width of the fabric unless otherwise indicated. Borders include extra length for "insurance" and will be trimmed after assembling quilt top center. All measurements include ¹/₄" seam allowances.*

From green print fabric:
- Cut 2 *lengthwise* **side outer borders** 3" x 77¹/₄".
- Cut 2 *lengthwise* **top/bottom outer borders** 3" x 82¹/₄".

From yellow print fabric:
- Cut 2 *lengthwise* **side middle borders** 2¹/₂" x 73¹/₄".
- Cut 2 *lengthwise* **top/bottom middle borders** 2¹/₂" x 77¹/₄".

From red print fabric:
- Cut 2 *lengthwise* **side inner borders** 2¹/₂" x 69¹/₄".
- Cut 2 *lengthwise* **top/bottom inner borders** 2¹/₂" x 73¹/₄".

From dark blue, medium blue, light blue, red, dark pink, medium pink, light pink, olive green, dark green, medium green, and light green print fabrics:
- Cut 6 **strips** 2¹/₄"w from **each** fabric.

From orange, dark yellow, medium yellow, light yellow, and navy print fabrics:
- Cut 7 **strips** 2¹/₄"w from **each** fabric.
  - From 1 navy strip and 1 dark yellow strip, cut 4 **squares** 2¹/₄" x 2¹/₄".
  - From 1 medium yellow strip and 1 light yellow strip, cut 8 **squares** 2¹/₄" x 2¹/₄".
  - From 1 orange strip, cut 1 **center square** 2¹/₄" x 2¹/₄".

ASSEMBLING THE QUILT TOP

*Follow **Piecing**, page 86, and **Pressing**, page 87, to assemble the quilt top.*

1. Sew strips together in color order shown to make **Strip Set 1**. Make 6 **Strip Set 1's**.
2. With right sides together and matching long raw edges, sew final lengthwise seam of **Strip Set 1** to form a tube (**Fig. 1**). Repeat with remaining Strip Set 1's.

Strip Set 1
(make 6)

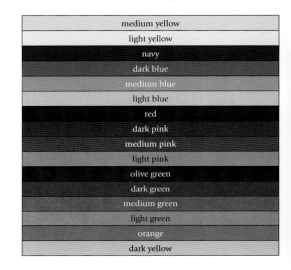

Fig. 1

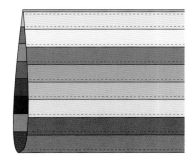

3. Referring to **Fig. 2**, cut across Strip Sets at 2¹/₄" intervals to make 84 circular **Strip Units**.

4. Referring to **Section** diagrams, working from top to bottom, and laying strips horizontally on a flat surface, determine where to remove stitching from **Strip Unit** (**Fig. 3**). Carefully arrange and sew **Strip Units** in correct order to make **Section A**. Make 2 **Section A's**.

5. In same manner, arrange and sew **Strip Units** in correct order to make **Section B**. Make 2 **Section B's**.

Fig. 2

Strip Unit
(make 84)

Fig. 3

Section A
(make 2)

Section B
(make 2)

6. Laying strips vertically, carefully remove seam and arrange and sew **Strip Units** in correct order to make **Section C**. Make 2 **Section C's**. Arrange and sew **Strip Units** in correct order to make **Section D**. Make 2 **Section D's**.

7. Sew 1 medium yellow, 2 light yellow, and 1 navy **square** together to make each **Section E**. Make 4 **Section E's**.

8. Use a seam ripper to remove seam between medium yellow and dark yellow squares of one **Strip Unit**. To make **Section F**, sew 1 dark yellow **square** to 1 end of **Strip Unit**. Sew 1 medium yellow **square** to opposite end of **Strip Unit**. Make 4 **Section F's**.

9. Refer to **Assembly Diagram** to sew **Sections** together to make quilt top center.

10. Follow **Adding Squared Borders**, page 88, to add **side**, then **top** and **bottom inner borders** to center section. Repeat to add **middle** and **outer borders** to complete **Quilt Top**.

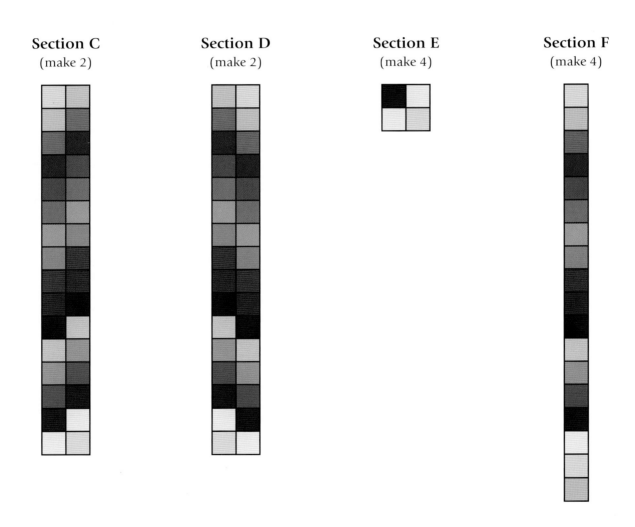

Section C
(make 2)

Section D
(make 2)

Section E
(make 4)

Section F
(make 4)

COMPLETING THE QUILT

1. Follow **Quilting**, page 89, to mark, layer, and quilt. Our quilt is hand quilted in diagonal lines across the pieced-square section and in the ditch along each border.

2. Cut a 30" square of binding fabric. Follow **Binding**, page 93, to bind quilt using $2^1/_2$"w continuous bias binding with overlapped corners.

Assembly Diagram

pineapple

If you've ever created a Log Cabin block, you know how much fun it is to watch alternating strips build into a colorful design. With the Pineapple Block, you essentially do the same thing—adding pieces to a central square—but with very different results. Because this quilt uses foundation piecing, you don't have to worry about accurate cutting before you sew. The sewing lines on the paper foundation will guide you to make perfect seams.

FINISHED BLOCK SIZE:
15" x 15" (38 cm x 38 cm)

FINISHED QUILT SIZE:
76" x 91" (193 cm x 231 cm)

YARDAGE REQUIREMENTS

Yardage is based on 43"/44"
(109 cm/112 cm) wide fabric.

- $7^1/_2$ yds (6.9 m) of cream solid fabric
- $3^1/_4$ yds (3 m) of red solid fabric
- $3^1/_4$ yds (3 m) of green solid fabric
- 7 yds (6.4 m) of fabric for backing
- 1 yd (91 cm) of fabric for binding
- 84" x 99" (213 cm x 251 cm) rectangle of batting

You will also need:

- 30 pieces of tracing paper $15^1/_2$" x $15^1/_2$" (39 cm x 39 cm)

CUTTING THE PIECES

*Follow **Rotary Cutting**, page 85, to cut fabric. Cut all strips across the selvage-to-selvage width of the fabric. All measurements include $^1/_4$" seam allowances. Due to variations in individual work and the nature of paper piecing, the actual number of strips needed may vary.*

From cream solid fabric:
- Cut 12 strips 7"w. From these strips, cut 60 squares 7" x 7". Cut squares once diagonally to make 120 **corner triangles**.
- Cut 90 **strips** $1^3/_4$" wide.

From red solid fabric:
- Cut 2 strips $2^5/_8$"w. From these strips, cut 30 **center squares** $2^5/_8$" x $2^5/_8$".
- Cut 60 **strips** $1^3/_4$" wide.

From green solid fabric:
- Cut 60 **strips** $1^3/_4$" wide.

MAKING THE PAPER FOUNDATION

1. To make a full-size paper foundation from pattern, page 26, use a ruler to draw a line down the center of a piece of tracing paper. Turn paper 90° and draw a second line down the center perpendicular to the first line. Place paper over pattern, matching grey lines of pattern to intersecting lines on paper. Trace pattern. Turn paper and trace pattern in each remaining corner. Do not cut out.

Block Diagram

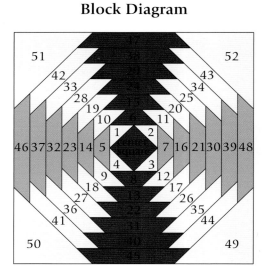

2. To make foundations, stack up to 12 sheets of paper together and pin pattern on top, being careful not to pin over traced lines. Use an unthreaded sewing machine with stitch length set at approximately 8 stitches per inch to sew over traced lines of pattern, perforating the paper through all layers. These perforated lines will be your sewing lines. Trim foundation to approximately $^1/_4$" from outer line. Refer to **Block Diagram** and transfer corresponding numbers to each foundation. Repeat to make a total of 30 foundations.

ASSEMBLING THE QUILT TOP

1. (**Note:** *Refer to **Block Diagram** for color placement. Numbers are not shown on **Figs. 1-4**.*) Place 1 **center square** right side up over center square area on numbered side of 1 **foundation**. Hold foundation up to a light to make sure enough fabric extends beyond the center square outline (sewing line) for seam allowance; pin in place (**Fig. 1**).

Fig. 1

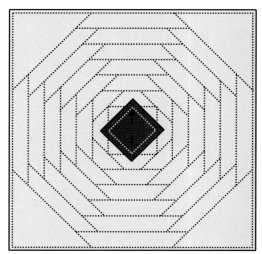

2. To cover area 1 on foundation, refer to **Fig. 2** to place 1 cream **strip** wrong side up on **center square**. Turn foundation over to sew directly on top of sewing line between center square and area 1, extending stitching a few stitches beyond beginning and end of line. Turn over to fabric side (**Fig. 2**).

3. Trim strip even with ends of stitching. Trim seam allowance to a scant $^1/_4$" if necessary (**Fig. 3**); open out strip. Make sure enough fabric extends beyond adjacent seamlines for seam allowance and trim off corners. Press and pin strip to foundation.

4. Repeat Steps 2 and 3 for areas 2, 3, and 4 (**Fig. 4**).

5. Referring to **Block Diagram**, repeat Steps 2 and 3 to add **strips** for areas 5-48 and to add **corner triangles** for areas 49-52 in numerical order. Trim block $^1/_4$" from outer line of block outline on **foundation** to complete **Block**. Block should measure $15^1/_2$" x $15^1/_2$" including seam allowances. Make 30 **Blocks**.

6. Sew 5 **Blocks** together to make **Row**, page 27. Make 6 **Rows**.

7. Referring to **Quilt Top Diagram**, page 27, sew **Rows** together. Carefully tear away **foundations** before completing **Quilt Top**.

Fig. 2

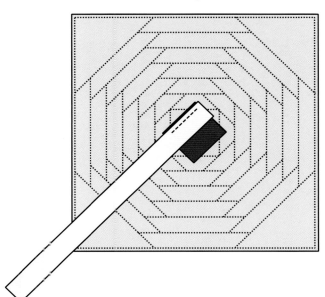

Fig. 3

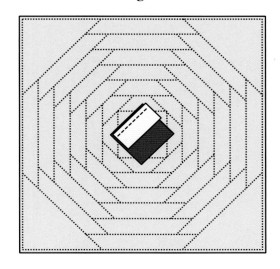

Fig. 4

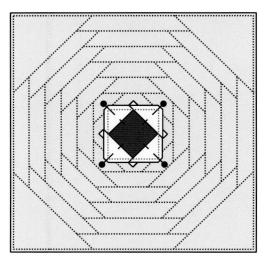

Block
(make 30)

COMPLETING THE QUILT TOP

1. Follow **Quilting**, page 89, to mark, layer, and outline quilt along each seamline. Our quilt is hand quilted.

2. Cut a 32" square of binding fabric. Follow **Binding**, page 93, to bind quilt using $2^1/_2$"w continuous bias binding with mitered corners.

$^1/_4$ Foundation Pattern

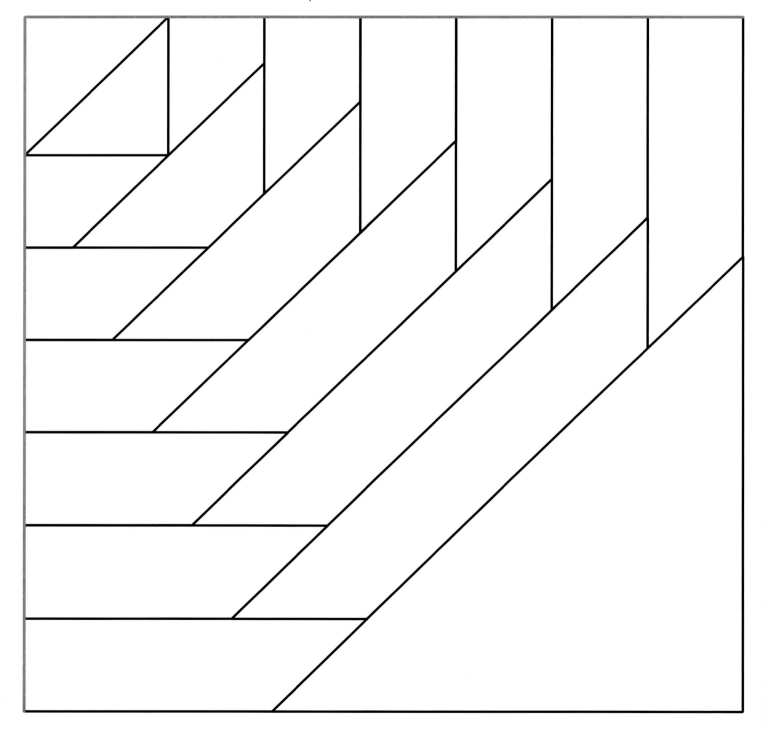

Row
(make 6)

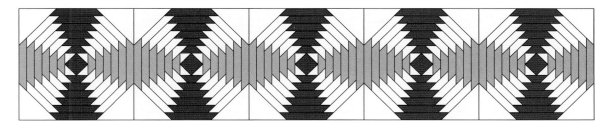

Quilt Top Diagram

true lover's knot

It's easy to imagine this romantic quilt being made for newlyweds in the time of the Great Depression. Perhaps it was finished at a quilting bee by the bride's mother, grandmother, aunts, friends— everyone who wanted to add their good wishes for the young couple's happiness. The main block is a four-patch featuring curved piecing. The small nine-patch blocks at the intersections of the sashing help create the appearance of connecting ribbons.

FINISHED BLOCK SIZE:
12" x 12" (30 cm x 30 cm)

FINISHED QUILT SIZE:
79" x 95½" (201 cm x 243 cm)

YARDAGE REQUIREMENTS

Yardage is based on 43"/44"
(109 cm/112 cm) wide fabric.

- 5³/₄ yds (5.3 m) of red solid fabric
- 4³/₄ yds (4.3 m) of white solid fabric
- 7¹/₄ yds (6.6 m) of fabric for backing
- 1 yd (91 cm) of fabric for binding
- 87" x 104" (221 cm x 264 cm) rectangle of batting

CUTTING THE PIECES

*Follow **Template Cutting** and **Rotary Cutting**, page 85, to cut fabric. All measurements include ¹/₄" seam allowances.*

From red solid fabric:
- Cut 38 **strips** 2" wide.
- Cut 6 strips 2" wide. From these strips, cut 120 **squares** 2" x 2".
- Cut 120 **A**'s using **Template A** pattern, page 33.
- Cut 60 **B**'s using **Template B** pattern, page 33.

From white solid fabric:
- Cut 22 **strips** 2" wide.
- Cut 6 strips 2" wide. From these strips, cut 120 **squares** 2" x 2".
- Cut 120 **A**'s using **Template A** pattern.
- Cut 60 **B**'s using **Template B** pattern.

ASSEMBLING THE QUILT TOP

*Follow **Piecing**, page 86, and **Pressing**, page 87, to assemble the quilt top.*

1. Sew 1 **A** and 2 **squares** together to make **Unit 1**. Make 60 **Unit 1's**.

2. *(Note: To sew curved seams in Steps 2 and 3, match centers and pin at center and at each end, then match and pin between pins. Sew seam with convex edge on bottom next to feed dogs.)* Sew 1 **A** and 1 **B** together to make **Unit 2**. Make 60 **Unit 2's**.

3. Sew **Unit 1** and **Unit 2** together to make **Unit 3**. Make 60 **Unit 3's**.

4. Repeat Steps 1-3 to make 60 **Unit 4's**.

5. Sew **Unit 3** and **Unit 4** together to make **Unit 5**. Make 60 **Unit 5's**.

6. Sew 2 **Unit 5's** together to make **Block**. Make 30 **Blocks**.

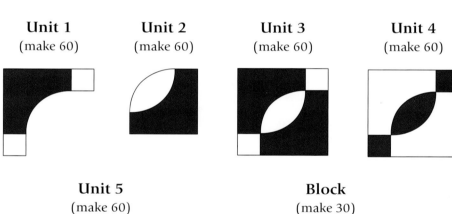

Unit 1
(make 60)

Unit 2
(make 60)

Unit 3
(make 60)

Unit 4
(make 60)

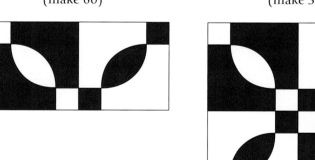

Unit 5
(make 60)

Block
(make 30)

7. Sew strips together to make Strip Set A. Make 18 Strip Set A's. Cut across 17 Strip Set A's at 12½' intervals to make 49 Sashing Units. Cut across remaining Strip Set A at 2" intervals to make 20 Unit 6's.

8. Sew strips together to make Strip Set B. Make 2 Strip Set B's. Cut across Strip Set B's at 2" intervals to make 40 Unit 7's.

9. Sew 1 Unit 6 and 2 Unit 7's together to make Unit 8. Make 20 Unit 8's.

10. Sew 5 Blocks and 4 Sashing Units together to make Row. Make 6 Rows.

11. Sew 5 Sashing Units and 4 Unit 8's together to make Sashing Row. Make 5 Sashing Rows.

12. Referring to Quilt Top Diagram, page 32, sew Rows and Sashing Rows together to complete Quilt Top.

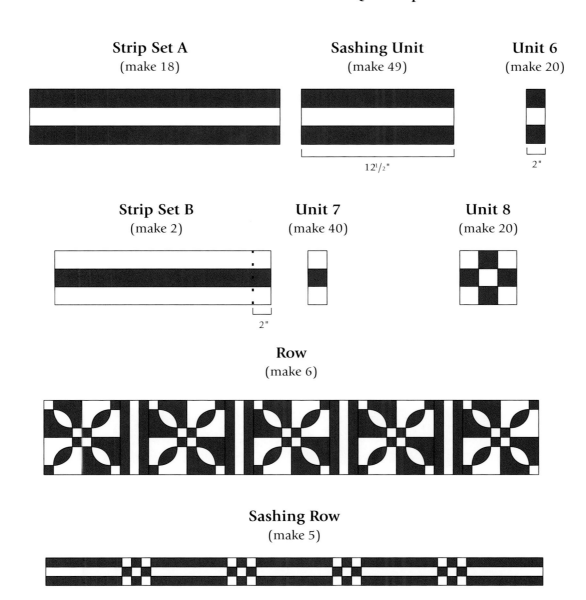

Strip Set A
(make 18)

Sashing Unit
(make 49)

12½"

Unit 6
(make 20)

2"

Strip Set B
(make 2)

2"

Unit 7
(make 40)

Unit 8
(make 20)

Row
(make 6)

Sashing Row
(make 5)

COMPLETING THE QUILT

1. Follow **Quilting**, page 89, to mark, layer, and quilt using **Quilting Diagram** as a suggestion. Our quilt is hand quilted.

2. Cut a 32" square of binding fabric. Follow **Binding**, page 93, to bind quilt using $2^1/_2$"w continuous bias binding with mitered corners.

Quilt Top Diagram

Quilting Diagram

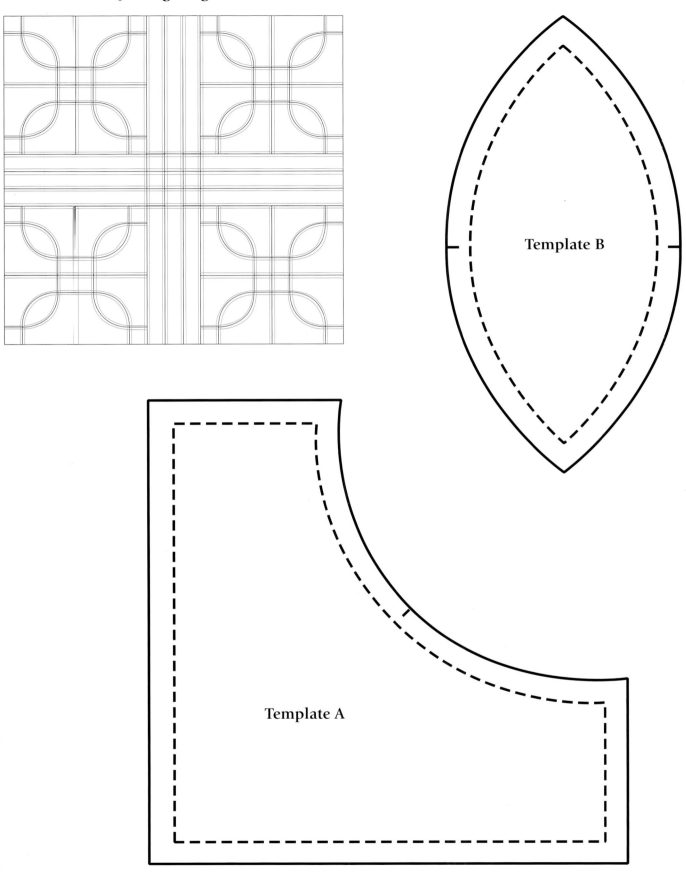

Template B

Template A

hourglasses and geese

This crisp blue-and-white quilt combines the simple four-triangle Hourglass block with Flying Geese sashing. These two designs are some of the most common components of quilt making. The Hourglass block is also called Bowtie or X block. If you begin looking for it, you will see it as a smaller unit in other popular blocks, such as Ohio Star or Crosses-and-Losses. Getting perfect points on the Flying Geese is easy with the stitch-and-flip technique. It also speeds the process of creating this refreshing quilt top.

FINISHED BLOCK SIZE:
8¼" x 8¼" (21 cm x 21 cm)

FINISHED QUILT SIZE:
80¾" x 91¾" (205 cm x 233 cm)

YARDAGE REQUIREMENTS

Yardage is based on 43"/44"
(109 cm/112 cm) wide fabric.

- 6³/₄ yds (6.2 m) of cream print fabric
- 6¹/₄ yds (5.7 m) of blue solid fabric
- 7¹/₂ yds (6.9 m) of fabric for backing
- 1 yd (91 cm) of fabric for binding
- 89" x 100" (226 cm x 254 cm) rectangle of batting

CUTTING THE PIECES

*Follow **Rotary Cutting**, page 85, to cut fabric. Cut all strips across the selvage-to-selvage width of the fabric. All measurements include ¹/₄" seam allowances.*

From cream print fabric:
- Cut 7 strips 9⁵/₈"w. From these strips, cut 28 **large squares** 9⁵/₈" x 9⁵/₈".
- Cut 87 strips 1⁷/₈"w. From these strips, cut 1812 **small squares** 1⁷/₈" x 1⁷/₈".

From blue solid fabric:
- Cut 7 strips 9⁵/₈"w. From these strips, cut 28 **large squares** 9⁵/₈" x 9⁵/₈".
- Cut 44 strips 3¹/₄"w. From these strips, cut 906 **rectangles** 1⁷/₈" x 3¹/₄".

ASSEMBLING THE QUILT TOP

*Follow **Piecing**, page 86, and **Pressing**, page 87, to assemble the quilt top.*

1. Draw a diagonal line on wrong side of each cream print **large square**. With right sides together place 1 cream print large square on top of 1 blue solid **large square**. Stitch seam ¹/₄" from each side of drawn line (**Fig. 1**).

2. Cut along drawn line and press seam allowances to darker fabric to make 2 **Triangle-Squares**. Make 56 **Triangle-Squares**.

3. Referring to **Fig. 2**, place 2 **triangle-squares** right sides and opposite colors together, matching seams. Referring to **Fig. 3**, draw a diagonal line. Stitch ¹/₄" from each side of line. Cut apart on drawn line and press open to make 2 **Blocks**. Repeat with remaining **triangle-squares** to make a total of 56 **Blocks**. Trim each Block to 8³/₄" x 8³/₄".

4. Place 1 **small square** on 1 **rectangle** and stitch diagonally as shown in **Fig. 4**. Trim ¹/₄" from stitching line as shown in **Fig. 5**. Press open, pressing seam allowance toward darker fabric.

5. Place 1 **small square** on opposite end of **rectangle**. Stitch diagonally as shown in **Fig. 6**. Trim ¹/₄" from stitching line as shown in **Fig. 7**. Press open, pressing seam allowance toward darker fabric to make **Unit 1**.

6. Repeat Steps 4 and 5 using remaining **small squares** and **rectangles** to make a total of 906 **Unit 1's**.

7. Sew 6 **Unit 1's** together to make **Sashing Unit**. Make 127 **Sashing Units**.

8. Sew 2 **Unit 1's** together to make **Sashing Square**. Make 72 **Sashing Squares**.

Fig. 1   **Triangle-Square**   **Fig. 2**
(make 56)

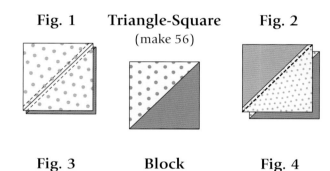

Fig. 3   **Block**   **Fig. 4**
(make 56)

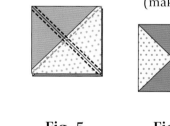
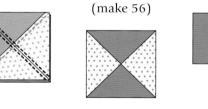

Fig. 5   **Fig. 6**   **Fig. 7**

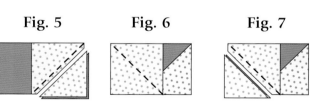

Unit 1   **Sashing Unit**   **Sashing Square**
(make 906)   (make 127)   (make 72)

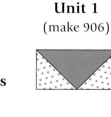

9. Sew 8 **Sashing Squares** and 7 **Sashing Units** together to make **Sashing Row**. Make 9 **Sashing Rows**.

10. Sew 8 **Sashing Units** and 7 **Blocks** together to make **Row**. Make 8 **Rows**.

11. Referring to **Quilt Top Diagram**, sew **Sashing Rows** and **Rows** together to complete **Quilt Top**.

Sashing Row

(make 9)

Row

(make 8)

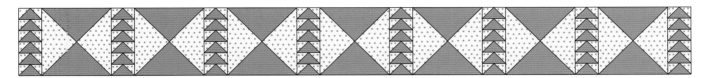

COMPLETING THE QUILT TOP

1. Follow **Quilting**, page 89, to mark, layer, and quilt using **Quilting Diagram** as a suggestion. Our quilt is hand quilted.

2. Cut a 32" square of binding fabric. Follow **Binding**, page 93, to bind quilt using $2^1/_2$"w continuous bias binding with mitered corners.

Quilting Diagram

Quilt Top Diagram

churn dash maze

The Churn Dash block has been appearing on quilts for more than 160 years. On some quilts, it's an equal nine-patch block, meaning its nine units are all the same size. In this Churn Dash Maze quilt, the block is an unequal nine patch with half-square triangles that are larger than the other pieces. The creator of this two-color quilt chose to set her blocks together with a fun sashing design called Garden Maze.

FINISHED BLOCK SIZE:
11¼" x 11¼" (29 cm x 29 cm)

FINISHED QUILT SIZE:
73½" x 90¼" (187 cm x 229 cm)

YARDAGE REQUIREMENTS

Yardage is based on 43"/44" (109 cm/112 cm) wide fabric.

- 4$\frac{1}{2}$ yds (4.1 m) of cream solid fabric
- 4$\frac{3}{4}$ yds (4.3 m) of navy print fabric
- 6$\frac{7}{8}$ yds (6.3 m) of fabric for backing
- 1 yd (91 cm) of fabric for binding
- 82" x 98" (208 cm x 249 cm) rectangle of batting

CUTTING THE PIECES

*Follow **Template Cutting** and **Rotary Cutting**, page 85, to cut fabric. Cut all strips across the selvage-to-selvage width of the fabric. All measurements include $\frac{1}{4}$" seam allowances.*

From cream solid fabric:
- Cut 6 strips 5$\frac{1}{2}$" wide. From these strips, cut 40 **squares** 5$\frac{1}{2}$" x 5$\frac{1}{2}$".
- Cut 4 strips 4$\frac{3}{4}$"w. From these strips, cut 30 squares 4$\frac{3}{4}$" x 4$\frac{3}{4}$". Cut squares twice diagonally to make 120 **triangles**.
- Cut 17 **wide strips** 4" wide.
- Cut 9 **strips** 2$\frac{3}{4}$" wide.

From navy print fabric:
- Cut 6 strips 5$\frac{1}{2}$" wide. From these strips, cut 40 **squares** 5$\frac{1}{2}$" x 5$\frac{1}{2}$".
- Cut 7 **strips** 2$\frac{3}{4}$" wide.
- Cut 34 **narrow strips** 1$\frac{1}{2}$" wide.
- Cut 60 **A's** using **Template A** pattern, page 42.
- Cut 30 **B's** using **Template B** pattern, page 42.

ASSEMBLING THE QUILT TOP

*Follow **Piecing**, page 86, and **Pressing**, page 87, to assemble the quilt top.*

1. Draw a diagonal line on wrong side of each cream solid **square**. With right sides together place 1 cream solid square on top of 1 navy print **square**. Stitch seam $\frac{1}{4}$" from each side of drawn line (**Fig. 1**).
2. Cut along drawn line and press seam allowances to darker fabric to make 2 **Triangle-Squares**. Make 80 **Triangle-Squares**. Trim each Triangle-Square to 5" x 5".
3. Sew 2 **strips** together to make **Strip Set A**. Make 3 Strip Set A's. Cut across **Strip Set A's** at 2$\frac{3}{4}$" intervals to make 40 **Unit 1's**.
4. Sew 5 **strips** together to make **Strip Set B**. Make 2 **Strip Set B's**. Cut across **Strip Set B's** at 2$\frac{3}{4}$" intervals to make 20 **Unit 2's**.

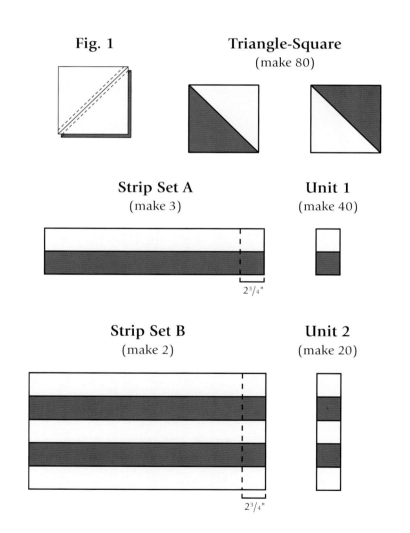

Fig. 1

Triangle-Square
(make 80)

Strip Set A
(make 3)

Unit 1
(make 40)

2$\frac{3}{4}$"

Strip Set B
(make 2)

Unit 2
(make 20)

2$\frac{3}{4}$"

5. Sew 2 **triangle-squares** and 1 **Unit 1** together to make **Unit 3**. Make 40 **Unit 3's**.
6. Sew 2 **Unit 3's** and 1 **Unit 2** together to make **Block**. Make 20 **Blocks**.
7. Sew 1 **wide** and 2 **narrow strips** together to make **Strip Set C**. Make 17 **Strip Set C's**. Cut across **Strip Set C's** at 11³/₄" intervals to make 49 **Sashing Units**.
8. Sew 2 **triangles** and 1 **A** together to make **Unit 4**. Make 60 **Unit 4's**.
9. Sew 2 **Unit 4's** and 1 **B** together to make **Sashing Square**. Make 30 **Sashing Squares**.
10. Sew 5 **Sashing Squares** and 4 **Sashing Units** together to make **Sashing Row**. Make 6 **Sashing Rows**.
11. Sew 5 **Sashing Units** and 4 **Blocks** together to make **Row**. Make 5 **Rows**.
12. Referring to Quilt Top Diagram, page 43, sew **Sashing Rows** and **Rows** together to complete **Quilt Top**.

Unit 3
(make 40)

Block
(make 20)

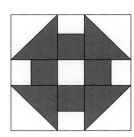

Strip Set C
(make 17)

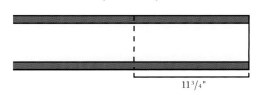

11³/₄"

Sashing Unit
(make 49)

Unit 4
(make 60)

Sashing-Square
(make 30)

Sashing Row
(make 6)

Row
(make 5)

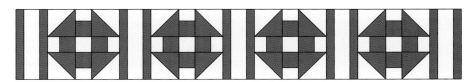

COMPLETING THE QUILT TOP

1. Follow **Quilting**, page 89, to mark, layer, and quilt using **Quilting Diagram** as a suggestion. Our quilt is hand quilted.
2. Cut a 32" square of binding fabric. Follow **Binding**, page 93, to bind quilt using 2^1/$_2$"w continuous bias binding with mitered corners.

Quilting Diagram

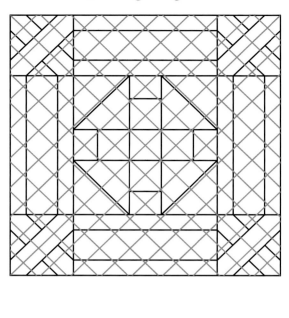

Template B

Template A

Quilt Top Diagram

mariner's compass

The Mariner's Compass is one of the oldest quilt designs that historians have identified. In the 1700s when the multi-pointed design appeared, patchwork quilting was in its infancy. It is believed the design was inspired by the wind roses found on old compasses and sea charts, although it wasn't commonly called "Mariner's Compass" until much later. This admirable quilt pattern includes oak leaf appliqués and a Sawtooth sashing and inner border.

FINISHED BLOCK SIZE:
21" x 21" (53 cm x 53 cm)

FINISHED QUILT SIZE:
89" x 105⅜" (226 cm x 268 cm)

YARDAGE REQUIREMENTS

Yardage is based on 43"/44" (109 cm/112 cm) wide fabric.

- 4³/₄ yds (4.3 m) of ecru print fabric
- 5¹/₄ yds (4.8 m) of tan print fabric
- ³/₄ yd (69 cm) of light blue print fabric
- 2¹/₂ yds (2.3 m) of medium blue print fabric
- 5¹/₂ yds (5 m) of dark blue print fabric for blocks and borders
- 3⁵/₈ yds (3.3 m) of red print fabric
- 8¹/₈ yds (7.4 m) of fabric for backing
- 1¹/₈ yds (1 m) of fabric for binding
- 97" x 114" (246 cm x 290 cm) rectangle of batting

CUTTING THE PIECES

*Follow **Template Cutting** and **Rotary Cutting**, page 85, to cut fabric. Make templates for all patterns on pages 49-51. It is important to transfer dots to your templates and to fabric pieces. (**Note:** Patterns for appliqué templates **H** and **N** do not include seam allowances; add seam allowances to these pieces when they are cut out.) Borders include extra length for "insurance" and will be trimmed after assembling quilt top center.*

From ecru print fabric:
- Cut 320 **A**'s.
- Cut 312 **L**'s.
- Cut 40 **M**'s.

From tan print fabric:
- Cut 31 **G**'s.
- Cut 9 ¹/₂**G**'s (add ¹/₄" seam allowance to grey line).
- Cut 9 ¹/₂**G**'s (reversed).

From light blue print fabric:
- Cut 80 **E**'s.

From medium blue print fabric:
- Cut 160 **B**'s.
- Cut 31 **H**'s.
- Cut 9 ¹/₂**H**'s.
- Cut 9 ¹/₂**H**'s (reversed).
- Cut 7 **L**'s.
- Cut 2 **O**'s.
- Cut 6 **P**'s.

From dark blue print fabric:
- Cut 2 *lengthwise* **side outer borders** 10" x 90".
- Cut 2 *lengthwise* **top/bottom outer borders** 10" x 92⁵/₈".
- Cut 71 **D**'s.
- Cut 6 **F**'s.
- Cut 9 **I**'s.
- Cut 9 **I**'s (reversed).
- Cut 7 **J**'s.
- Cut 2 **K**'s.

From red print fabric:
- Cut 80 **C**'s.
- Cut 312 **L**'s.
- Cut 40 **N**'s.

ASSEMBLING THE QUILT TOP

*Follow **Piecing**, page 86, and **Pressing**, page 87, to assemble the quilt top. When piecing, carefully match dots and pin pieces together. Sew from fabric edge to fabric edge. To complete our quilt you will need 6 blocks, 7 half blocks, and 2 quarter blocks.*

1. Sew 1 **B** between 2 **A**'s to make **Unit 1**. Make a total of 16 **Unit 1**'s. Sew 1 **C** between 2 **Unit 1**'s to make **Unit 2**. Make a total of 8 **Unit 2**'s. Sew 1 **E** to 1 **D** to make **Unit 3**. Make a total of 8 **Unit 3**'s.

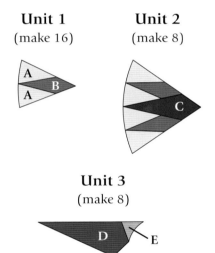

Unit 1
(make 16)

Unit 2
(make 8)

Unit 3
(make 8)

2. Follow **Unit 4** diagram and sew **Unit 2's** and **Unit 3's** together to make **Unit 4**. Follow **Sewing Curves**, page 87, and sew 1 **F** to **Unit 4** to make **Unit 5**.

3. Sew 4 **G's** together to make **Unit 6**.

4. Sew **Unit 5** to **Unit 6**. Follow **Hand Appliqué**, page 87, and appliqué 1 **H** to each corner to complete **Block**.

5. Repeat Steps 1-4 to make 6 **Blocks**.

6. For each half block, follow **Half Block** diagram and sew pieces together in same order as **Block**. Make 7 Half Blocks.

7. For each quarter block, follow **Quarter Block** diagram and sew pieces together in same order as **Block**. Make 2 Quarter Blocks.

8. For sashing, sew 8 ecru **L's** to 8 red **L's** to make **Unit 7**. Repeat to make a total of 20 **Unit 7's**.

9. Sew 1 **Unit 7** between 2 **M's** to make **Unit 8**. Hand appliqué 1 **N** to each **M**. Repeat to make a total of 20 **Unit 8's**.

Unit 4

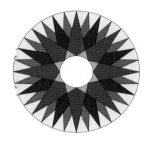

Unit 5

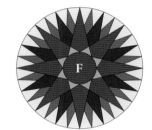

Unit 6

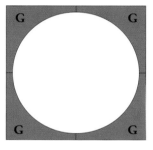

Block
(make 6)

Half Block
(make 7)

Quarter Block
(make 2)

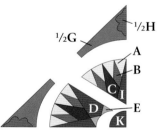

Unit 7
(make 20)

Unit 8
(make 20)

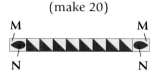

10. Follow **Assembly Diagram** to sew **Blocks**, **Half Blocks**, **Quarter Blocks**, **Unit 8's**, and medium blue **L's**, **O's**, and **P's** together.

11. For top inner border, sew 33 ecru **L's** to 33 red **L's**. Repeat to make bottom inner border.

12. For side inner border, sew 43 ecru **L's** to 43 red **L's**. Repeat to make 2 side inner borders.

13. Referring to **Quilt Top Diagram** and easing to fit, sew borders to pieced blocks to complete **Quilt Top**.

14. Follow **Adding Squared Borders**, page 88, to sew side outer borders, then top and bottom outer borders to quilt top.

Quilting Diagram

Assembly Diagram

COMPLETING THE QUILT TOP

1. Follow **Quilting**, page 89, to mark, layer, and quilt as desired using **Quilting Diagram** as a suggestion. Our quilt is hand quilted.
2. Cut a 34" square of binding fabric. Follow **Binding**, page 93, to bind quilt using $2^1/2$"w continuous bias binding with mitered corners.

Quilt Top Diagram

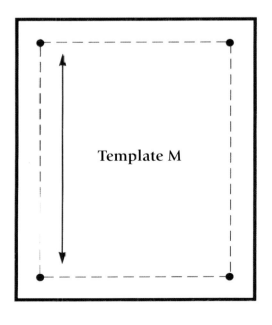

Template M

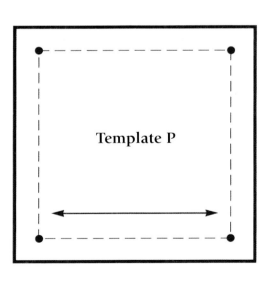

Template P

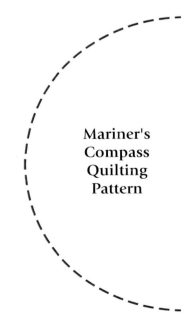

Mariner's Compass Quilting Pattern

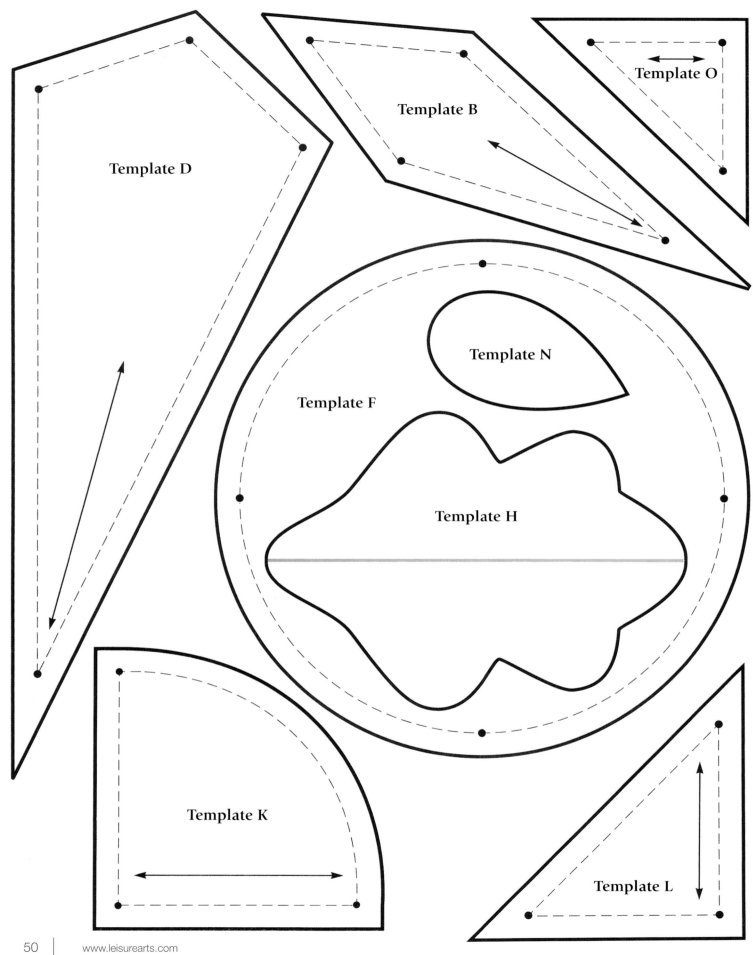

Template D

Template B

Template O

Template N

Template F

Template H

Template K

Template L

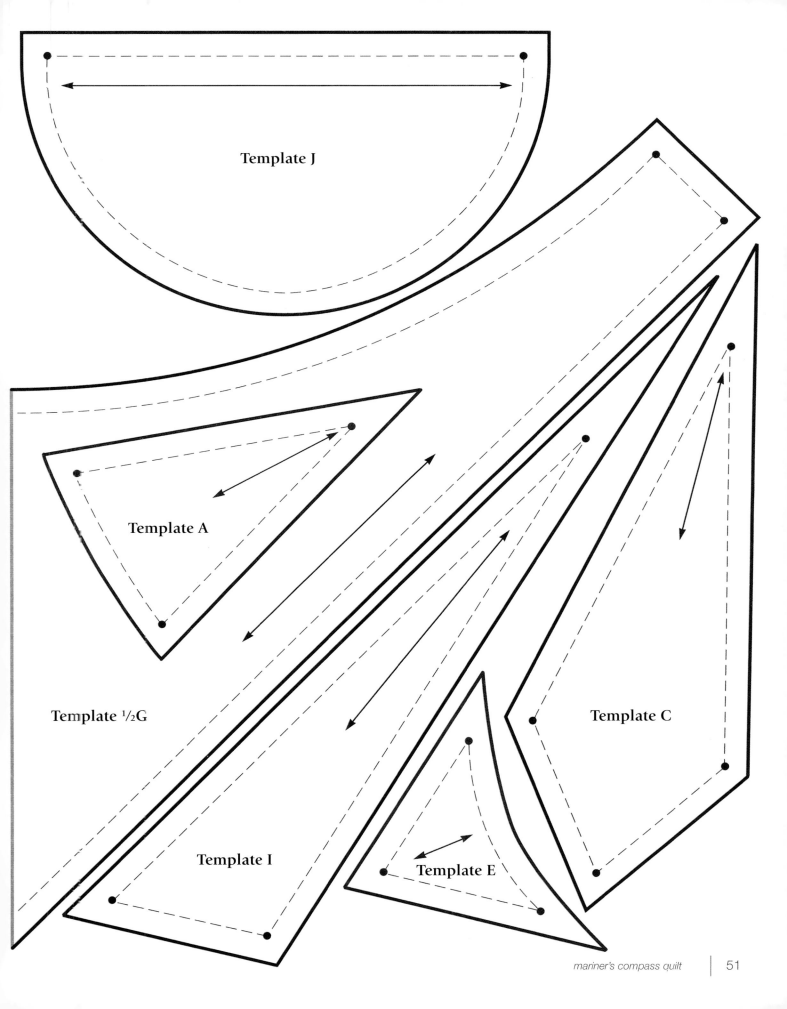

Template J

Template A

Template ½G

Template I

Template E

Template C

rail fence

It's hard to imagine an easier block to sew than Rail Fence. You just sew seven long strips side-by-side, then cut the large pieced unit into equal blocks. When choosing colors for your quilt, have fun. Pick the hues that appeal to you. The maker of this quilt used the print fabrics of the late nineteenth century.

FINISHED BLOCK SIZE:
$8^3/_4$" x $8^3/_4$" (22 cm x 22 cm)

FINISHED QUILT SIZE:
$76^1/_4$" x $76^1/_4$" (194 cm x 194 cm)

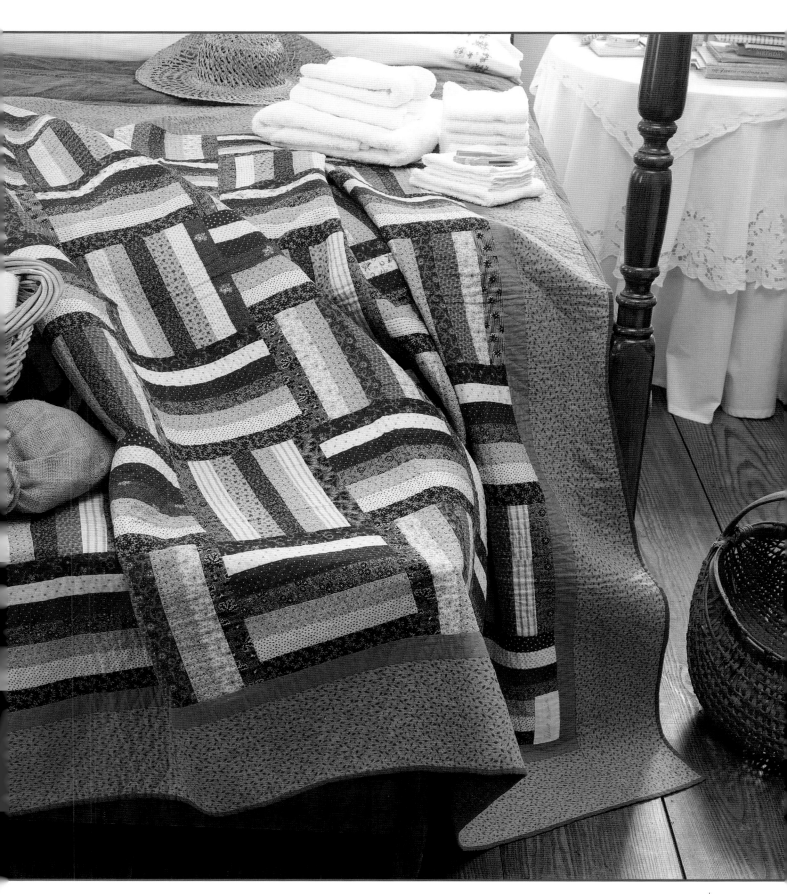

YARDAGE REQUIREMENTS

Yardage is based on 43"/44" (109 cm/112 cm) wide fabric.

- 1¹/₂ yds (1.4 m) **total** of assorted dark print fabrics
- 1¹/₂ yds (1.4 m) **total** of assorted light print fabrics
- 2¹/₈ yds (1.9 m) **total** of assorted medium print fabrics
- 2 yds (1.8 m) **total** of blue solid fabric
- 2¹/₄ yds (2.1 m) of pink print fabric
- 7¹/₈ yds (6.5 m) of fabric for backing
- 1 yd (91 cm) of fabric for binding
- 85" x 85" (216 cm x 216 cm) square of batting

CUTTING THE PIECES

Follow Rotary Cutting, page 85, to cut fabric. Cut all strips across the selvage-to-selvage width of the fabric unless otherwise indicated. Borders include extra length for "insurance" and will be trimmed after assembling quilt top center. All measurements include ¹/₄" seam allowances.

From assorted dark print fabrics:
- Cut 26 **strips** 1³/₄" wide.

From assorted light print fabrics:
- Cut 26 **strips** 1³/₄" wide.

From assorted medium print fabrics:
- Cut 39 **strips** 1³/₄" wide.

From blue solid fabric:
- Cut 2 *lengthwise* **top** and **bottom inner borders** 1³/₄" x 65³/₄".
- Cut 2 *lengthwise* **side inner borders** 1³/₄" x 68¹/₄".

From pink print fabric:
- Cut 2 *lengthwise* **top** and **bottom outer borders** 6¹/₄" x 68¹/₄".
- Cut 2 *lengthwise* **side outer borders** 6¹/₄" x 79³/₄".

ASSEMBLING THE QUILT TOP

Follow Piecing, page 86, and Pressing, page 87, to assemble the quilt top.

1. Referring to **Strip Set Diagram**, sew 2 **dark**, 2 **light**, and 3 **medium strips** together to make 1 **Strip Set**. Make 13 **Strip Sets**.
2. Cut across Strip Sets at 9¹/₄" intervals to make **Rail Fence Block**. Make 49 **Rail Fence Blocks**.
3. Referring to **Quilt Top Diagram** for orientation, sew 7 **Rail Fence Blocks** together to make **Row**. Make 7 **Rows**.
4. Sew Rows together to make Quilt Top Center.
5. Follow **Adding Squared Borders**, page 88, to sew **top** and **bottom inner borders**, then **side inner borders** to center section. Repeat to add **outer borders** to center section to complete piecing the **Quilt Top**.

Strip Set
(make 13)

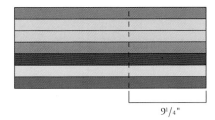

9¹/₄"

Rail Fence Block
(make 49)

COMPLETING THE QUILT TOP

1. Follow **Quilting**, page 89, to mark, layer, and quilt as desired. Our quilt is hand quilted with alternating parallel diagonal or vertical straight lines in the blocks. The borders are quilted with diagonal channel quilting.

2. Cut a 30" square of binding fabric. Follow **Binding**, page 93, to bind quilt using $2^1/_2$"w continuous bias binding with mitered corners.

Quilt Top Diagram

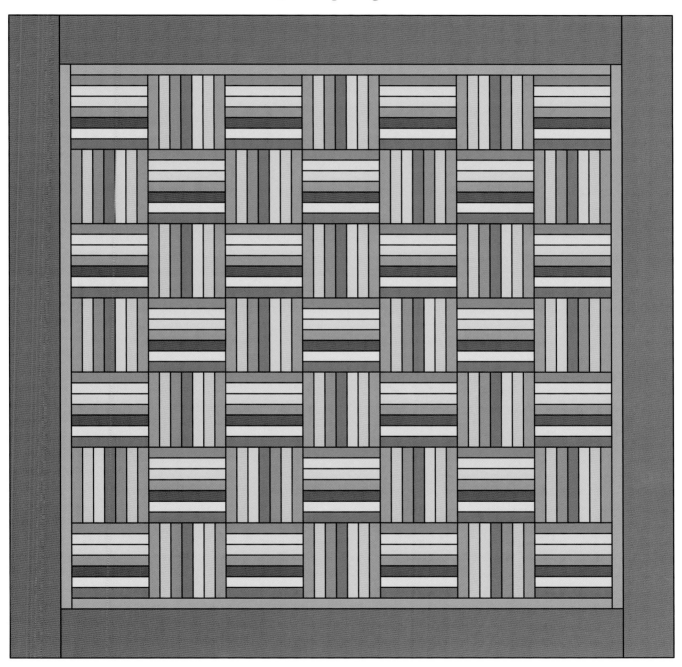

building blocks

Also known as Baby Blocks and Tumbling Blocks, this eye-catching quilt has the illusion of depth, created by the use of three colors. The pieces are easy to cut with a rotary cutter and ruler. The classic quilt shown uses all diamonds, but to avoid awkward set-in seams, our instructions use diamonds and triangles pieced into triangle units. By matching like-colored triangles, you create a quilt top that is one continuous treat for the eyes.

FINISHED QUILT SIZE:
96" x 112" (244 cm x 284 cm)

YARDAGE REQUIREMENTS

Yardage is based on 43"/44"
(109 cm/112 cm) wide fabric.

- 6¼ yds (5.7 m) of dark blue print fabric
- 4⁷⁄₈ yds (4.5 m) of blue print fabric
- 3³⁄₈ yds (3.1 m) of light blue print fabric
- 8³⁄₄ yds (8 m) of fabric for backing
- 1¹⁄₈ yds (1 m) of fabric for binding
- 104" x 120" (264 cm x 305 cm) rectangle of batting

CUTTING THE PIECES

*Follow **Rotary Cutting**, page 85, to cut fabric. Cut all strips across the selvage-to-selvage width of the fabric unless otherwise indicated. Borders include extra length for "insurance" and will be trimmed after assembling quilt top center. All measurements include ¹⁄₄" seam allowances.*

From dark blue print fabric:
- Cut 13 **wide strips** 3¹⁄₄" wide.
- Cut 22 **narrow strips** 3" wide.
- Cut 4 *lengthwise* **outer borders** 8" x 104".

From blue print fabric:
- Cut 22 **narrow strips** 3" wide.
- Cut 2 *lengthwise* **side inner borders** 3" x 99".
- Cut 2 *lengthwise* **top/ bottom inner borders** 3" x 89".
- From remaining fabric width, cut 19 *crosswise* **wide strips** 3¹⁄₄" wide.

From light blue print fabric:
- Cut 13 **wide strips** 3¹⁄₄" wide.
- Cut 22 **narrow strips** 3" wide.

ASSEMBLING THE QUILT TOP

*Follow **Piecing**, page 86, and **Pressing**, page 87, to assemble the quilt top.*

1. Referring to **Fig. 1**, align 60° marking on ruler (shown in pink) with lower edge of 1 dark blue **narrow strip**. Cut along right side of ruler to cut 1 end of strip at a 60° angle.
2. Turn cut **strip** 180° on mat and align 60° marking on ruler with lower edge of strip. Align previously cut 60° edge with 3" marking on ruler. Cut strip at 3" intervals as shown in **Fig. 2** to cut diamonds.
3. Repeat Steps 1 and 2 using remaining dark blue, blue, and light blue **narrow strips** to cut a total of 220 **dark blue diamonds**, 220 **blue diamonds**, and 220 **light blue diamonds**.

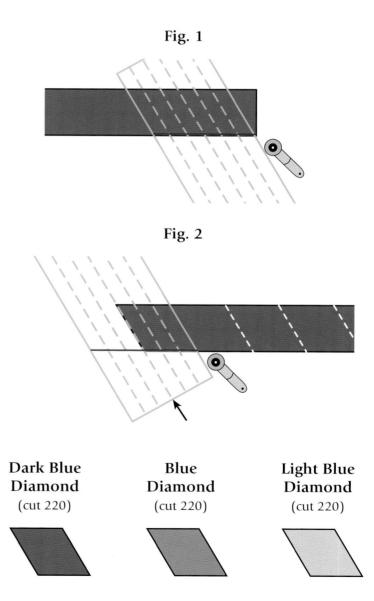

Fig. 1

Fig. 2

Dark Blue Diamond	**Blue Diamond**	**Light Blue Diamond**
(cut 220)	(cut 220)	(cut 220)

4. Cutting diamonds at
   3¹/₄" intervals, repeat
   Steps 1 and 2 using dark
   blue, blue, and light blue
   wide strips to cut a total of
   110 **dark blue diamonds**,
   110 **blue diamonds**, and
   110 **light blue diamonds**.
   Referring to **Fig. 3**, cut across
   diamonds (cut in Step 4) to
   make a total of 220 **dark blue
   triangles**, 220 **blue triangles**,
   and 220 **light blue triangles**.
5. Sew 1 **blue diamond**, 1 **dark
   blue triangle**, and 1 **light
   blue diamond** together
   to make **Unit 1**. Make
   220 **Unit 1's**.
6. Sew 1 **light blue triangle**,
   1 **dark blue diamond**, and
   1 **blue triangle** together
   to make **Unit 2**. Make
   220 **Unit 2's**.
7. Sew 1 **Unit 1** and 1 **Unit 2**
   together to make **Unit 3**.
   Make 220 **Unit 3's**.
8. Referring to **Assembly
   Diagram**, page 60, and
   rotating Unit 3's as needed,
   sew 22 **Unit 3's** together to
   make 1 vertical row. Make
   10 vertical rows; sew rows
   together.
9. To trim top and bottom edges
   straight, refer to **Fig. 4** to
   line up ¹/₄" marking on ruler
   (shown in pink) with seam
   intersections. Trim off excess
   to make center section of
   quilt top.
10. Follow **Adding Squared
    Borders**, page 88, to sew **side**,
    then **top** and **bottom inner
    borders** to center section.
    Repeat to add **outer borders**
    to complete **Quilt Top**.

Fig. 3

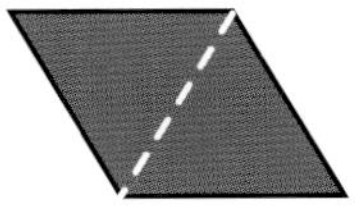

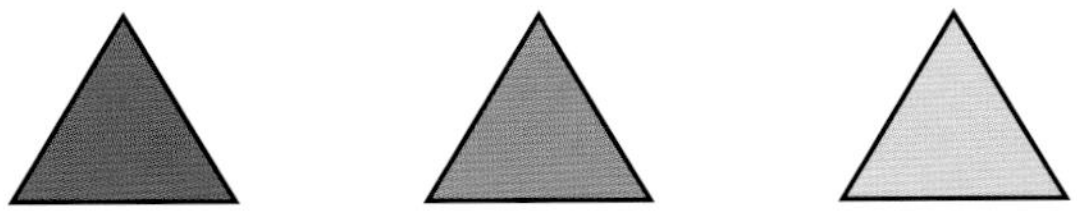

**Dark Blue
Triangle**
(cut 220)

**Blue
Triangle**
(cut 220)

**Light Blue
Triangle**
(cut 220)

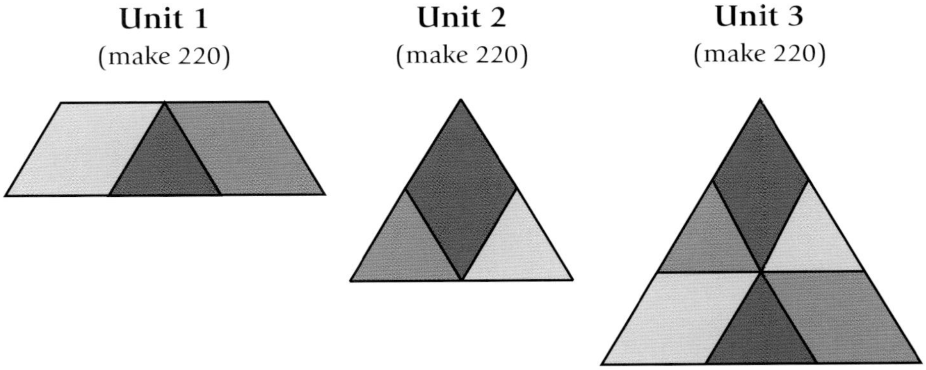

Unit 1
(make 220)

Unit 2
(make 220)

Unit 3
(make 220)

Fig. 4

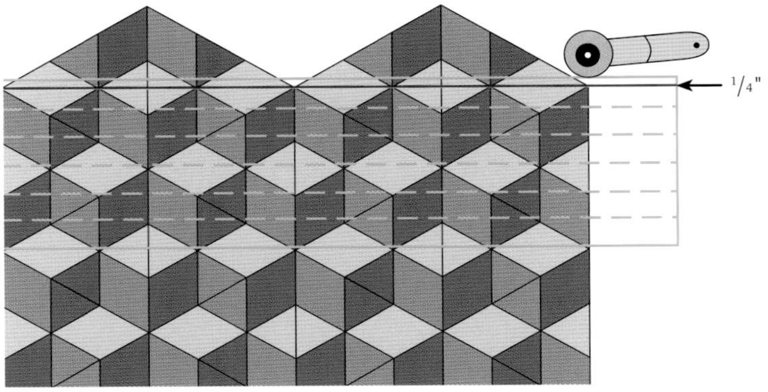

Quilting Diagram

COMPLETING THE QUILT TOP

1. Follow **Quilting**, page 89, to mark, layer, and quilt, using **Quilting Diagram**, page 59, as a suggestion. Our quilt is hand quilted.

2. Cut a 35" square of binding fabric. Follow **Binding**, page 93, to bind quilt using $2^1/_2$"w continuous bias binding with overlapped corners.

Assembly Diagram

Quilt Top Diagram

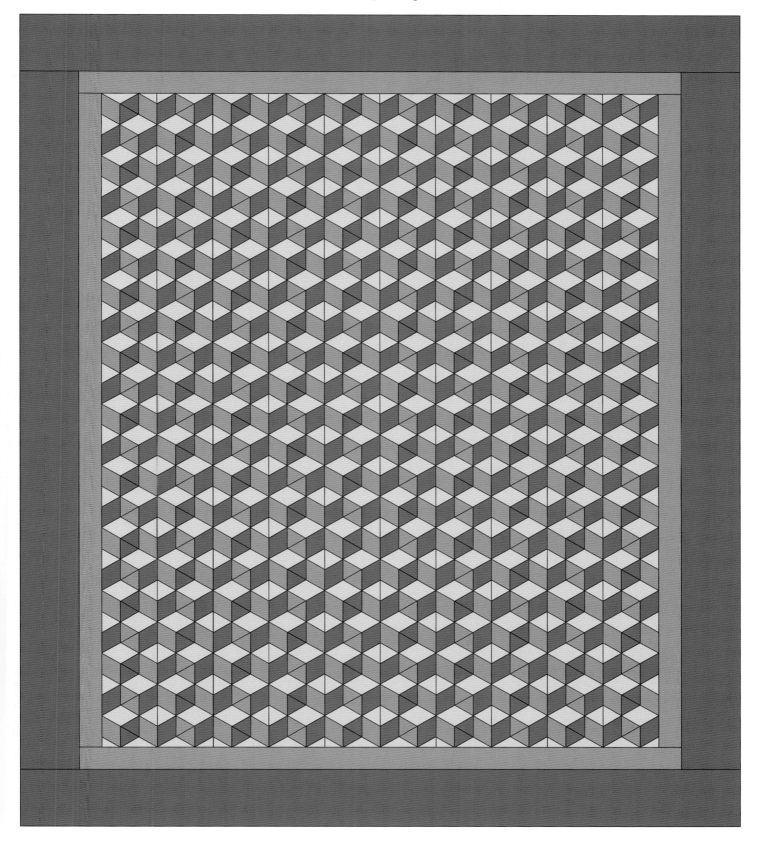

tree of life

The Bible is a source of many American quilt block names, and these blocks can vary widely, with entirely different patterns sharing the same name. This is true of Tree of Life blocks. Most are pieced "on point." They can have two, three, four, or more rows of "leaves." The blocks in this particular quilt are unusual because a small strip of red fabric rather than a solid triangle indicates the ground beneath the tree.

FINISHED BLOCK SIZE:
9$^1/_4$" x 9$^1/_4$" (23 cm x 23 cm)

FINISHED QUILT SIZE:
69" x 86" (175 cm x 218 cm)

*We simplified the piecing of this quilt by substituting solid setting triangles for the half blocks used on the edges of our antique quilt (see **Assembly Diagram**, page 66). We also resized the too-small quilt to fit a traditional twin-size bed.*

YARDAGE REQUIREMENTS

Yardage is based on 43"/44" (109 cm/112 cm) wide fabric.

4$^3/_8$ yds (4 m) of red solid fabric
2$^1/_4$ yds (2.1 m) of cream solid fabric
2 yds (1.8 m) of green solid fabric
5$^1/_4$ yds (4.8 m) of fabric for backing
1 yd (91 cm) of fabric for binding
77" x 94" (196 cm x 239 cm) square of batting

CUTTING THE PIECES

*Follow **Rotary Cutting**, page 85, to cut fabric. Cut all strips across the selvage-to-selvage width of the fabric unless otherwise indicated. Borders include extra length for "insurance" and will be trimmed after assembling quilt top center. All measurements include $^1/_4$" seam allowances.*

From red solid fabric:

- Cut 2 strips 14$^3/_8$"w. From these strips, cut 4 squares 14$^3/_8$" x 14$^3/_8$". Cut squares twice diagonally to make 16 **setting triangles** (you will need 14 and have 2 left over).
- Cut 3 strips 3$^1/_4$"w. From these strips, cut 31 **sashing squares** 3$^1/_4$" x 3$^1/_4$".
- Cut 16 strips 1$^1/_2$"w. From these strips, cut 32 **short borders** 1$^1/_2$" x 8$^3/_4$" and 32 **long borders** 1$^1/_2$" x 9$^3/_4$".
- Cut 4 strips 1$^1/_2$"w. From these strips, cut 32 **trunks** 1$^1/_2$" x 4$^1/_2$".
- Cut 1 strip 5$^1/_8$"w. From this strip, cut 5 squares 5$^1/_8$" x 5$^1/_8$". Cut squares twice diagonally to make 20 **sashing triangles** (you will need 18 and have 2 left over).
- Cut 3 strips 6$^3/_8$"w. From these strips, cut 16 squares 6$^3/_8$" x 6$^3/_8$". Cut squares once diagonally to make 32 **large triangles**.
- Cut 2 strips 2"w. From these strips, cut 32 **large squares** 2" x 2".
- Cut 18 strips 2$^3/_8$"w. From these strips, cut 288 **very large squares** 2$^3/_8$" x 2$^3/_8$" for triangle-squares.
- Cut 2 squares 7$^1/_2$" x 7$^1/_2$". Cut squares once diagonally to make 4 **corner setting triangles**.

From cream solid fabric:

- Cut 4 strips 1$^7/_8$"w. From these strips, cut 64 **medium squares** 1$^7/_8$" x 1$^7/_8$".
- Cut 1 strip 1$^1/_4$"w. From these strip, cut 32 **small squares** 1$^1/_4$" x 1$^1/_4$".
- Cut 3 strips 6"w. From these strips, cut 16 squares 6" x 6". Cut squares twice diagonally to make 64 **small triangles**.
- Cut 18 strips 2$^3/_8$"w. From these strips, cut 288 **very large squares** 2$^3/_8$" x 2$^3/_8$" for triangle-squares.

From green solid fabric:

- Cut 20 strips 3$^1/_4$"w. From these strips, cut 80 **sashing strips** 3$^1/_4$" x 9$^3/_4$".

ASSEMBLING THE QUILT TOP

*Follow **Piecing**, page 86, and **Pressing**, page 87, to assemble the quilt top.*

1. Draw a diagonal line on wrong side of each cream **very large square**. With right sides together place 1 cream very large square on top of 1 red **very large square**. Stitch seam $^1/_4$" from each side of drawn line (**Fig. 1**).

2. Cut along drawn line and press seam allowances to darker fabric to make 2 **Triangle-Squares**. Make 576 **Triangle-Squares**. Trim each Triangle-Square to 1$^7/_8$" x 1$^7/_8$".

Fig. 1

Triangle-Square
(make 576)

3. Sew 10 **triangle-squares** and 2 **medium squares** together to make **Unit 1**. Make 32 **Unit 1's**.

4. Sew 8 **triangle-squares** together to make **Unit 2**. Make 32 **Unit 2's**.

5. Sew 1 **large triangle**, 1 **Unit 2**, and 1 **Unit 1** together to make **Unit 3**. Make 32 **Unit 3's**.

6. Referring to **Fig. 2a** and **2b**, sew 1 **trunk** and 2 **small triangles** together. Trim trunk even with triangles to make **Unit 4**. Make 32 **Unit 4's**.

7. Matching right sides and raw edges, place 1 **small square** and 1 **large square** together. Sew diagonally across **small square (Fig. 3a)**. Trim ¹/₄" beyond stitching **(Fig. 3b)** and press open to make **Unit 5**. Make 32 **Unit 5's**.

8. Matching right sides and raw edges, place 1 **Unit 5** and 1 **Unit 4** together. Sew diagonally across **Unit 5 (Fig. 4a)**. Trim ¹/₄" beyond stitching **(Fig. 4b)** and press open to make **Unit 6**. Make 32 **Unit 6's**.

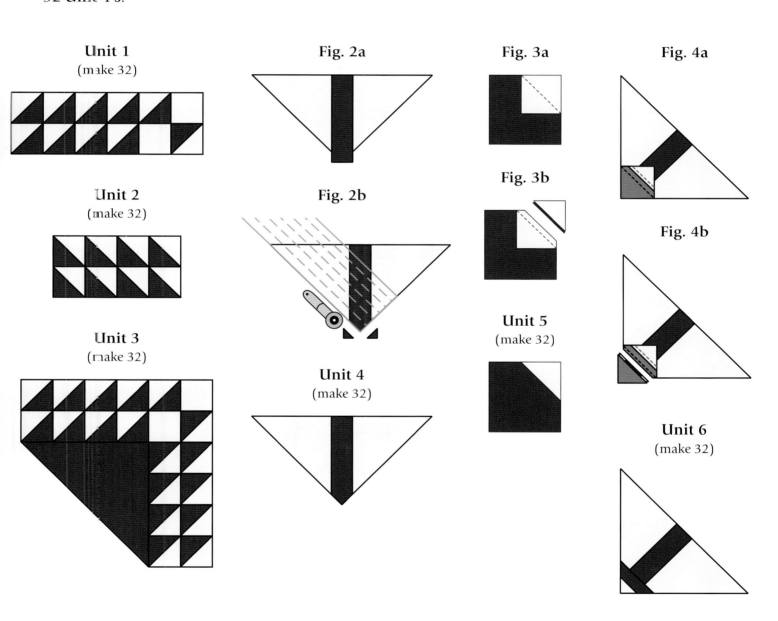

Unit 1
(make 32)

Unit 2
(make 32)

Unit 3
(make 32)

Fig. 2a

Fig. 2b

Unit 4
(make 32)

Fig. 3a

Fig. 3b

Unit 5
(make 32)

Fig. 4a

Fig. 4b

Unit 6
(make 32)

9. Sew 1 **Unit 3** and 1 **Unit 6** together to make **Unit 7**. Make 32 **Unit 7's**.

10. Sew **short**, then **long borders** to **Unit 7** to complete **Block**. Make 32 **Blocks**.

11. Referring to **Assembly Diagram**, sew **corner setting triangles**, **sashing triangles**, **sashing strips**, **setting triangles**, **sashing squares**, and **Blocks** together into **Rows**. Sew **Rows** together to complete **Quilt Top**.

Unit 7
(make 32)

Block
(make 32)

COMPLETING THE QUILT TOP

1. Follow **Quilting**, page 89, to mark, layer, and quilt using **Quilting Diagram** as a suggestion. Our quilt is hand quilted.

2. Cut a 31" square of binding fabric. Follow **Binding**, page 93, to bind quilt using $2^1/2$"w continuous bias binding with mitered corners.

Quilting Diagram

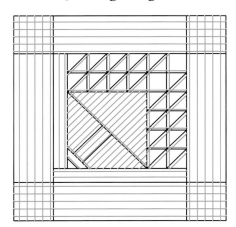

Assembly Diagram

log cabin wall hanging

The bold colors of this Amish-style wall hanging will add warmth to any surroundings. Log Cabin blocks are classic! They're perfect for beginning quilters and an excellent opportunity for anyone who likes to work with contrasting-color fabrics. With their half-dark/half-light appearance, Log Cabin blocks are a lot of fun to arrange into different patterns. This particular block setting is usually called "Barn Raising."

FINISHED BLOCK SIZE:
$5^3/_4$" x $5^3/_4$" (15 cm x 15 cm)

FINISHED WALL HANGING SIZE:
$38^1/_2$" x 50" (98 cm x 127 cm)

YARDAGE REQUIREMENTS

Yardage is based on 43"/44"
(109 cm/112 cm) wide fabric.

- 2 yds (1.8 m) of black solid fabric
- $1^1/4$ yds (1.1 m) of blue solid fabric
- $1/8$ yd (11 cm) **each** of 24 assorted medium solids (***Note:** Colors may be repeated for more than 1 Block.*)
- $3^1/4$ yds (3 m) of fabric for backing
- $3/4$ yd (69 cm) of fabric for binding
- $46^1/2$" x 58" (118 cm x 147 cm) rectangle of batting

CUTTING THE PIECES

*Follow **Rotary Cutting**, page 85, to cut fabric. Cut all strips across the selvage-to-selvage width of the fabric unless otherwise indicated. Borders include extra length for "insurance" and will be trimmed after assembling quilt top center. All measurements include $1/4$" seam allowances.*

From black solid fabric:
- Cut 18 **strips** $1^1/4$" wide.
- Cut 2 *lengthwise* **side outer borders** $5^1/2$" x $43^1/2$".
- Cut 2 *lengthwise* **top/bottom outer borders** $5^1/2$" x 32".
- From remaining width, cut 3 strips $1^3/4$"w. From these strips, cut 24 **squares** $1^3/4$" x $1^3/4$".

From blue solid fabric:
- Cut 2 *lengthwise* **side inner borders** $2^3/4$" x $43^1/2$".
- Cut 2 *lengthwise* **top/bottom inner borders** $2^3/4$" x $27^1/2$".
- From remaining width, cut 1 strip $5^1/2$"w. From this strip, cut 4 **corner squares** $5^1/2$" x $5^1/2$".

From *each* of 24 assorted medium solids:
- Cut 1 **strip** $1^1/4$" wide.

ASSEMBLING THE WALL HANGING TOP

*Follow **Piecing**, page 86, and **Pressing**, page 87. Use a $1/4$" seam allowance.*

1. Matching right sides and raw edges, place 1 medium solid **strip** and 1 black **square** together. Stitch as shown in **Fig. 1**. Trim strip even with square (**Fig. 2**); press open (**Fig. 3**).
2. Turn **square** $1/4$ turn counter clockwise and repeat Step 1 to add the next "log" as shown in **Figs. 4-6**.
3. Repeat Step 2 to add black **strips** to remaining 2 sides of **square** (**Fig. 7**).

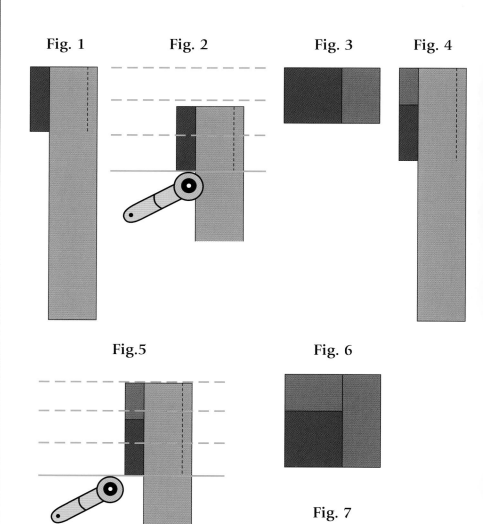

Fig. 1   Fig. 2   Fig. 3   Fig. 4

Fig.5   Fig. 6

Fig. 7

4. Continue adding **strips**, alternating 2 medium solid strips and 2 black strips until there are 3 strips on each side of square to make **Block**.

5. Using remaining strips, repeat Steps 1-4 to make a total of 24 **Blocks**.

6. Referring to **Wall Hanging Top Diagram**, sew **Blocks** together into **Rows**. Sew **Rows** together to make center section of wall hanging top.

7. Follow **Adding Squared Borders**, page 88, to sew **top**, **bottom**, then **side inner borders** to center section.

8. Measure length of wall hanging top center across center of quilt. Trim side outer borders to determined length. Measure width of wall hanging center across center of quilt. Trim top/bottom outer borders to determined length.

9. Sew side outer borders to sides of wall hanging top center. Sew 1 corner square to each end of each top and bottom outer border. Sew top and bottom borders to wall hanging top.

Block
(make 24)

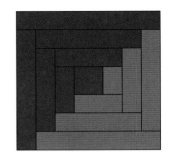

COMPLETING THE WALL HANGING

1. Follow **Quilting**, page 89, to mark, layer, and quilt, using **Quilting Diagram** as a suggestion. Our wall hanging is hand quilted.

2. Cut a 24" square of binding fabric. Follow **Binding**, page 93, to bind quilt using 2¹/₂"w continuous bias binding with overlapped corners.

Wall Hanging Top Diagram

Quilting Diagram

grandmother's flower garden

The hexagonal pieces of Grandmother's Flower Garden have charmed quilters since the 1930s. In an era when even tiny bits of fabric scraps were saved and reused, this design was a favorite. Quilters who love hand piecing will enjoy the English paper piecing method used to create this design. The paper templates ensure accurate piecing and make this a portable project.

FINISHED BLOCK SIZE:
$12^{1}/_{8}$" x 11" (31 cm x 28 cm)

FINISHED QUILT SIZE:
77" x $97^{3}/_{4}$" (196 cm x 248 cm)

YARDAGE REQUIREMENTS

Yardage is based on 43"/44" (109 cm/112 cm) wide fabric.

- ³/₈ yd (34 cm) of yellow solid fabric
- ¹/₈ yd (11 cm) **each** of 53 different print fabrics
- 6" x 9" (15 cm x 23 cm) scrap of coordinating solid for **each** print
- 4⁵/₈ yds (4.2 m) of green solid fabric
- 3⁵/₈ yds (3.3 m) of white solid fabric
- 7¹/₈ yds (6.5 m) of fabric for backing
- ⁷/₈ yd (80 cm) of fabric for binding
- 85" x 106" (216 cm x 269 cm) rectangle of batting

You will also need:

- 1" (2.54 cm) pre-cut paper hexagons (see page 76)

CUTTING THE PIECES

*Follow **Rotary Cutting**, page 85, to cut fabric. Cut all strips across the selvage-to-selvage width of the fabric unless otherwise indicated. All measurements include ¹/₄" seam allowances.*

From yellow solid fabric:
- Cut 4 strips 2¹/₄" wide. From these strips, cut 53 **rectangles** 2¹/₄" x 2⁵/₈".

From *each* print fabric:
- Cut 1 strip 2¹/₄" wide. From this strip, cut 12 **rectangles** 2¹/₄" x 2⁵/₈".

From *each* scrap of solid fabric:
- Cut 2 strips 2¹/₄" wide. From these strips, cut 6 **rectangles** 2¹/₄" x 2⁵/₈".

From green solid fabric:
- Cut 66 strips 2¹/₄" wide. From these strips, cut 978 **rectangles** 2¹/₄" x 2⁵/₈".

From white solid fabric:
- Cut 52 strips 2¹/₄" wide. From these strips, cut 766 **rectangles** 2¹/₄" x 2⁵/₈".

*After cutting the number of rectangles needed from each fabric, stack 4 rectangles. Center and pin a paper hexagon to top rectangle. Using a rotary cutter and small acrylic ruler and leaving a ¹/₄" seam allowance on each side, trim corners from rectangles as shown in **Cutting Diagram**. Repeat to trim all rectangles.*

Cutting Diagram

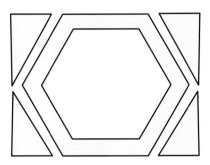

MAKING THE FLOWER BLOCKS

For each Flower Block you will need 1 yellow, 6 solid, 12 print, and 18 green hexagons.

1. Referring to **Fig. 1**, center paper **hexagon** on wrong side of fabric **hexagon**; fold and finger press top seam allowance back over paper.
2. Working counter clockwise and mitering fabric at the corner, fold top left seam allowance back over paper. Stitching from corner to corner and only through the fabric, use a long stitch to hold seam allowances in place (**Fig. 2**).

Fig. 1

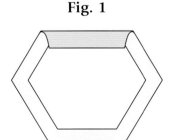

Fig. 2

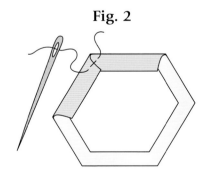

3. Referring to **Fig. 3**, continue to fold and stitch seam allowances, taking a backstitch at each corner. Repeat for each **hexagon** in **Flower Block**.

4. Matching right sides and corners, place yellow center and 1 solid **hexagon** together as shown in **Fig. 4**. Avoiding stitching through paper, and backstitching at beginning and end of seam, whipstitch edges together along one side. Open pieces flat (**Fig. 5**).

5. Whipstitching adjoining edges, continue adding solid **hexagons** one at a time until **Inner Ring** is completed. It is not necessary to knot and clip threads each time you reach the end of a **hexagon** side.

6. Add 12 print **hexagons** around **Inner Ring** until **Middle Ring** is completed.

7. To make **Outer Ring** and complete **Flower Block**, add 18 green **hexagons** around **Middle Ring**. Make a total of 53 **Flower Blocks**.

8. Carefully remove papers from center **hexagon**, **Inner Ring**, and **Middle Ring**. Leave papers in **Outer Ring** until each **hexagon** in the ring is completely attached to another hexagon.

9. Repeat **Steps 1-3** for all white and remaining 24 green **hexagons**.

10. Referring to **Assembly Diagram**, page 76, arrange **Flower Blocks** in **vertical Rows**. Use white and green **hexagons** as connectors to join **Blocks** into **Rows** and to join Rows together to complete **Quilt Top**.

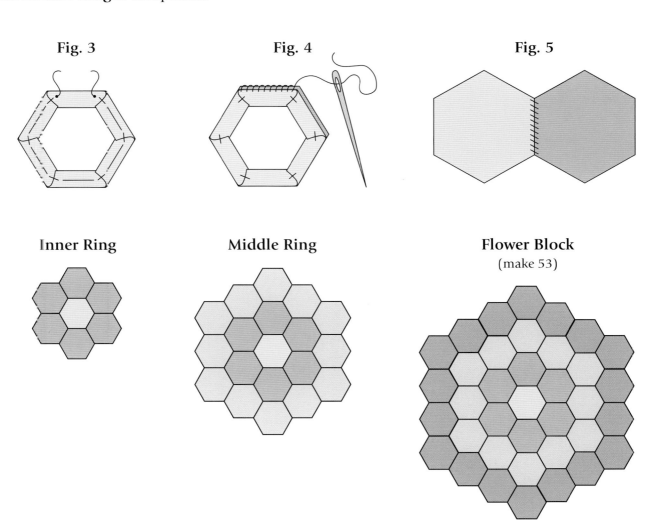

Fig. 3   **Fig. 4**   **Fig. 5**

Inner Ring   **Middle Ring**   **Flower Block**
(make 53)

COMPLETING THE QUILT

1. Follow **Quilting**, page 89, to mark, layer, and quilt as desired. Our quilt is hand quilted with outline quilting $1/8$" from the seams of each **hexagon**.

2. Referring to **Quilt Top Diagram** for placement, draw a cutting line around outside edge of quilt top. Stitch around edges of quilt $1/8$" inside drawn line. Trim edges of **Quilt Top**, backing, and batting along drawn line, being careful to only trim the protruding points of **hexagons**.

3. Follow **Making Continuous Bias Strip Binding**, page 93, Steps 1-7, and use a 30" square of binding fabric to make $1^1/4$"w bias binding.

4. Press 1 long edge of bias binding $1/4$" to wrong side. Press 1 short end of bias binding $1/2$" to wrong side. Matching right sides and raw edges and beginning with pressed end, sew binding to front of quilt, easing binding around curved edges until binding overlaps beginning end by approximately 2". Trim excess binding. Fold binding over to quilt backing and pin in place, covering stitching line. Blindstitch binding to backing.

Hexagon

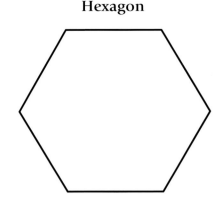

*Traditionally, one paper and one fabric hexagon are cut for each of the 2751 hexagons used in the quilt. To speed the cutting process, we used pre-cut paper hexagons and rotary cut the fabric hexagons. The paper hexagons can be reused up to 3 times, reducing the total needed to 917. **Hint:** Lightly spray starch and dry iron used hexagons before reuse.*

*If you choose to make freezer paper templates, refer to **Template Cutting**, page 85, to use hexagon pattern. Cut freezer paper into 138 sheets $8^1/2$" x 11".*

*Trace around template 20 times on dull side of 23 sheets. With 1 traced sheet on top and shiny sides down, stack 6 sheets of freezer paper together. To hold the sheets together, touch the tip of a hot iron to the center of each hexagon; cut out paper hexagons. Repeat with remaining sheets. Follow **Cutting the Pieces**, page 74, to cut fabric. Center hexagons, shiny side down, on the wrong side of each fabric rectangle and iron to rectangle; trim fabric corners as described in **Cutting Diagram**, page 74. Follow remainder of instructions to complete Quilt.*

Assembly Diagram

ocean waves

Blue and white—what better colors could there be for an Ocean Waves quilt? Not surprisingly, this pattern became popular on the New England coast. When the powerful Atlantic Ocean is your neighbor, it is only natural to want to name a quilt in its honor. What seems to be an intricate quilt pattern is actually formed by alternating quilt blocks, one of all triangle pieces, the other having a white square at its center.

FINISHED BLOCK SIZE:
8" x 8" (20 cm x 20 cm)

FINISHED QUILT SIZE:
84$\frac{1}{8}$" x 100$\frac{1}{8}$" (214 cm x 254 cm)

Our quick-and-easy prairie point instructions allow you to make continuous lengths of overlapping prairie points. The overlapping prairie points will look slightly different than the individual prairie points featured on the antique quilt in the photograph, pages 78-79.

YARDAGE REQUIREMENTS

Yardage is based on 43"/44" (109 cm/112 cm) wide fabric.
6⅝ yds (6.1 m) of white solid fabric
6¼ yds (5.7 m) of blue solid fabric
2⅛ yds (1.9 m) of fabric for prairie point edging
7¾ yds (7.1 m) of fabric for backing
92" x 108" (234 cm x 274 cm) rectangle of batting

CUTTING THE PIECES

Follow **Rotary Cutting**, *page 85, to cut fabric. Solid borders include extra length for "insurance" and will be trimmed after assembling quilt top center. All measurements include ¼" seam allowances.*

From white solid fabric:
- Cut 2 *lengthwise* strips 3½" x 90" for **side inner borders**.
- Cut 2 *lengthwise* strips 3½" x 74" for **top/bottom inner borders**.
- From remaining width, cut 8 strips 6⅛" wide. From these strips, cut a total of 31 **large squares** 6⅛" x 6⅛".
- From remaining width, cut 16 strips 2⅞" wide. From these strips, cut a total of 138 squares 2⅞" x 2⅞". Cut squares once diagonally to make 276 **small triangles**.
- Cut 2 strips 9¼" wide. From these strips, cut a total of 5 squares 9¼" x 9¼". Cut squares twice diagonally to make 20 **large triangles** (you will need 18 and have 2 left over).
- Cut 36 strips 3" wide. From these strips, cut 456 **small squares** 3" x 3" for triangle-squares.

From blue solid fabric:
- Cut 2 *lengthwise* strips 3½" x 102" for **side outer borders**.
- Cut 2 *lengthwise* strips 3½" x 86" for **top/bottom outer borders**.
- From remaining width, cut 15 strips 2⅞" wide. From these strips, cut a total of 134 squares 2⅞" x 2⅞". Cut squares once diagonally to make 268 **small triangles**.
- Cut 36 strips 3" wide. From these strips, cut 456 **small squares** 3" x 3" for triangle-squares.

From prairie point edging fabric:
- Cut 11 strips 6" wide. From these strips, cut 18 **long pieces** 6" x 19½" and 4 **short pieces** 6" x 10½".

ASSEMBLING THE QUILT TOP

*Follow **Piecing**, page 86, and **Pressing**, page 87, to assemble the quilt top.*

1. Draw a diagonal line on wrong side of each white solid **small square**. With right sides together place 1 white solid small square on top of 1 blue solid **small square**. Stitch seam ¹/₄" from each side of drawn line (**Fig. 1**).
2. Cut along drawn line and press seam allowances to darker fabric to make 2 **Triangle-Squares**. Make 912 **Triangle-Squares**. Trim each Triangle-Square to 2¹/₂" x 2¹/₂".
3. Assemble 4 **triangle-squares** as shown to make **Unit 1**. Make 160 **Unit 1's**.
4. Assemble 4 **Unit 1's** as shown to make **Block A**. Make 20 **Block A's**.
5. Assemble 2 **Unit 1's** as shown to make **Block B**. Make 14 **Block B's**.
6. Assemble 4 **Unit 1's** as shown to make **Block C**. Make 12 **Block C's**.
7. Assemble 1 **triangle-square** and 2 **small triangles** as shown to make **Unit 3**. Make 84 **Unit 3's**. Assemble 1 **triangle-square** and 2 **small triangles** as shown to make **Unit 4**. Make 80 **Unit 4's**.
8. Assemble 2 **Unit 3's**, 2 **Unit 4's**, and 1 **large square** as shown to make **Block D**. Make 31 **Block D's**.
9. Assemble 1 **Unit 4**, 1 **Unit 3**, and 1 **large triangle** as shown to make **Block E**. Make 18 **Block E's**.

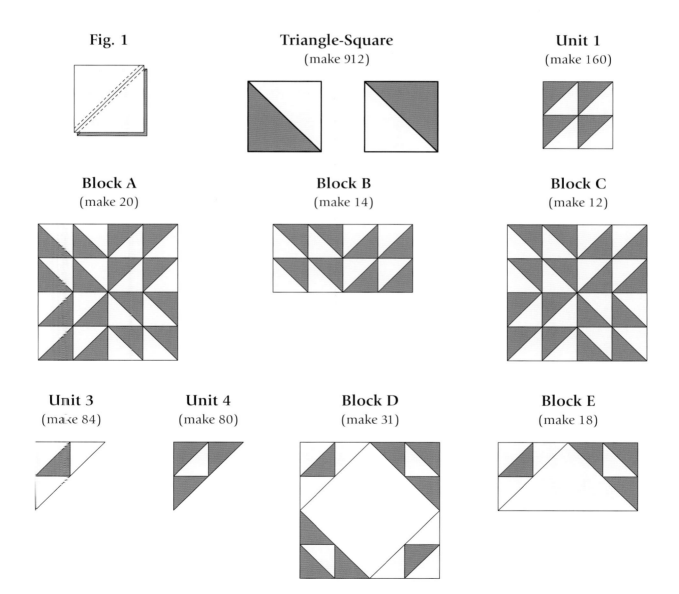

Fig. 1

Triangle-Square
(make 912)

Unit 1
(make 160)

Block A
(make 20)

Block B
(make 14)

Block C
(make 12)

Unit 3
(make 84)

Unit 4
(make 80)

Block D
(make 31)

Block E
(make 18)

10. Assemble 2 **Unit 1's**, 4 **Block E's**, and 3 **Block B's** as shown to make **Row A**. Make 2 **Row A's**.

11. Assemble 2 **Block E's**, 4 **Block A's**, and 3 **Block D's** as shown to make **Row B**. Make 5 **Row B's**.

12. Assemble 2 **Block B's**, 4 **Block D's**, and 3 **Block C's** as shown to make **Row C**. Make 4 **Row C's**.

13. Referring to **Quilt Top Diagram**, page 84, assemble **Rows** to complete center section of quilt top.

14. Follow **Adding Mitered Borders**, page 88, to attach **inner borders** to center section of quilt top.

15. Assemble 1 **triangle-square** and 2 **small triangles** as shown to make **Unit 5**. Make 108 **Unit 5's**.

16. Assemble 24 **Unit 5's** and 1 **Unit 3** as shown to make **Top/Bottom Pieced Border**. Make 2 **Top/Bottom Pieced Borders**.

17. Assemble 30 **Unit 5's** and 1 **Unit 3** as shown to make **Side Pieced Border**. Make 2 **Side Pieced Borders**.

18. Easing as needed, sew **Pieced Borders** to top, bottom, and sides of center section of quilt top, beginning and ending seams exactly ¹/₄" from each corner of quilt top and backstitching at beginning and end of stitching.

19. Fold 1 corner of quilt top diagonally with right sides together, matching outer edges of borders as shown in **Fig. 3**. Beginning at point where previous seams ended, stitch to outer corner. Repeat with remaining corners.

20. Follow **Adding Mitered Borders**, page 88, to attach **outer borders** to complete **Quilt Top**.

Row A
(make 2)

Row B
(make 5)

Row C
(make 4)

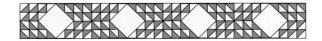

Unit 5
(make 108)

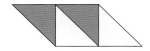

Top/Bottom Pieced Border
(make 2)

Side Pieced Border
(make 2)

Fig. 3

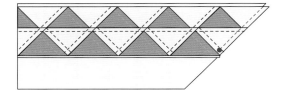

MAKING PRAIRIE POINT EDGING

1. Place 1 **long piece** wrong side up. Referring to **Fig. 4**, mark a line along center of piece. Beginning at left edge and above the center line, mark lines 3 ' apart. Beginning 1½" from the left edge and below the center line, mark lines 3" apart.
2. Referring to **Fig. 5**, use scissors to trim away 1½ ' wide sections and to cut along 3" drawn lines up to the center line.
3. Referring to **Fig. 6**, press first "square" to right of center line in half diagonally once; press in half diagonally again and pin to form prairie point (**Fig. 7**).
4. Press first "square" to left of center line in half diagonally once (**Fig. 8**). Press prairie point on right to the left along the center line; press second fold of triangle over first prairie point and pin to form second prairie point (**Fig. 9**).
5. Alternating from 1 side of the center line to the other, repeat Step 4 until all squares are folded to form prairie points. Stitch a scant ¼" from base of prairie points to complete **Prairie Point Unit**.
6. Repeat Step 1-5 with remaining **long** and **short pieces** to complete 18 **Long Prairie Point Units** and 4 **Short Prairie Point Units**.

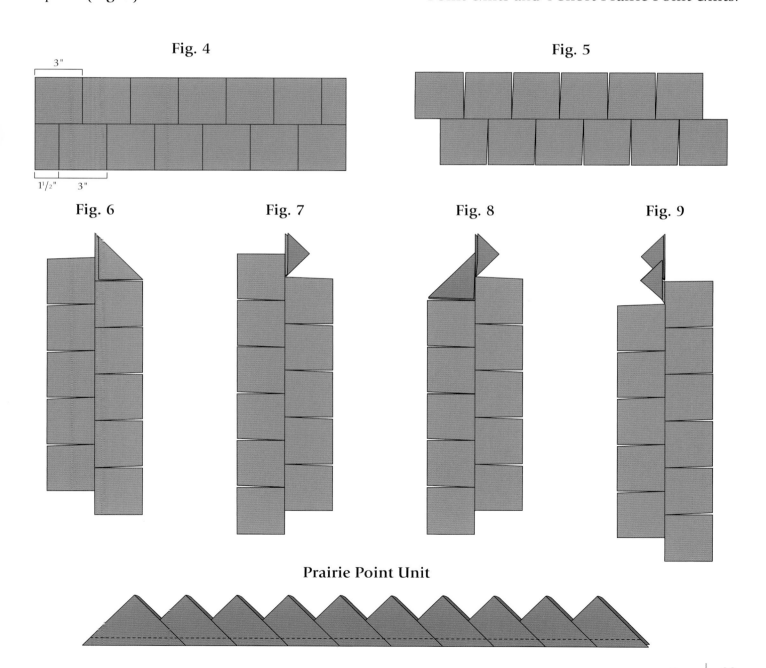

Fig. 4

3"

1½"   3"

Fig. 5

Fig. 6   **Fig. 7**   **Fig. 8**   **Fig. 9**

Prairie Point Unit

COMPLETING THE QUILT

1. Follow **Quilting**, page 89, and **Quilting Diagram**, to mark, layer, and quilt to within 1" from edges of quilt. Trim backing and batting even with quilt top.
2. Fold backing away from edges of quilt. Using 1 **Short Prairie Point Unit** and 4 **Long Prairie Point Units** for top and bottom edges and 1 **Short Prairie Point Unit** and 5 **Long Prairie Point Units** for each side edge, pin **Prairie Point Units** on right side along each edge of quilt top, overlapping and easing Units as necessary. Sew prairie points to quilt top and batting. Press prairie points away from center of quilt top.
3. Finger press edge of backing $1/4$" to wrong side. Covering raw edge of prairie points and stitching, blind stitch backing in place.

Quilting Diagram

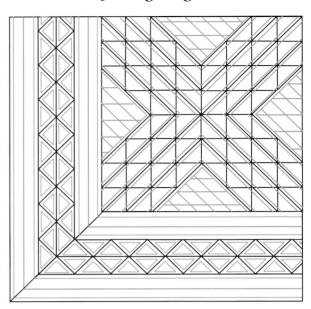

Quilt Top Diagram

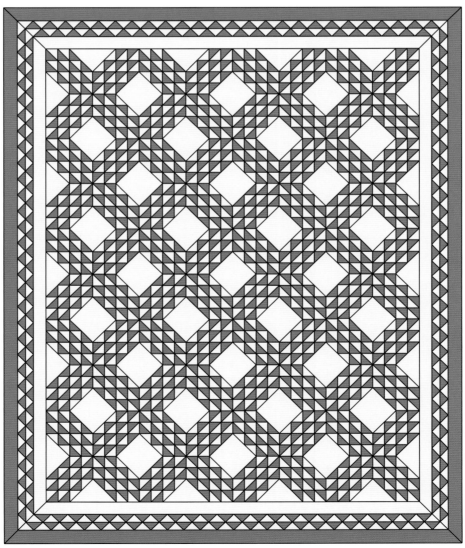

To make your quilting easier and more enjoyable, we encourage you to carefully read all of the general instructions, study the color photographs, and familiarize yourself with the individual project instructions before beginning a project.

FABRICS

SELECTING FABRICS

Choose high-quality, medium-weight 100% cotton fabrics. All-cotton fabrics hold a crease better, fray less, and are easier to quilt than cotton/polyester blends.

Yardage requirements listed for each project are based on 43"/44" wide fabric with a "usable" width of 40" after shrinkage and trimming selvages. Actual usable width will probably vary slightly from fabric to fabric. Our recommended yardage lengths should be adequate for occasional re-squaring of fabric when many cuts are required.

PREPARING FABRICS

We recommend that all fabrics be washed, dried, and pressed before cutting. If fabrics are not pre-washed, washing the finished quilt will cause shrinkage and give it a more "antiqued" look and feel. Bright and dark colors, which may run, should always be washed before cutting. After washing and drying fabric, fold lengthwise with wrong sides together and matching selvages.

TEMPLATE CUTTING

Our full-sized piecing template patterns have 2 lines – a solid cutting line and a dashed line showing the $^1/_4$" seam allowance. Patterns for appliqué templates do not include seam allowances.

1. To make a template from a pattern, use a permanent fine-point pen to carefully trace pattern onto template plastic, making sure to transfer all alignment and grainline markings. Cut out template along inner edge of drawn line. Check template against original pattern for accuracy.
2. To make a template from a one-quarter pattern, use a ruler to draw a line down the center of a sheet of template plastic. Turn plastic 90° and draw a line down the center, perpendicular to the first line. Match grey lines of pattern to intersection of lines on plastic. Trace pattern. Turn plastic and trace pattern in remaining corners. Cut out template as in Step 1.
3. To make a template from a one-half pattern, use a ruler to draw a line down the center of a sheet of template plastic. Match grey line of pattern to line on plastic. Trace pattern. Turn plastic 180° and trace pattern again. Cut out template as in Step 1.

4. To use a piecing template, place template on wrong side of fabric (unless otherwise indicated), aligning grainline on template with straight grain of fabric. Use a sharp fabric-marking pencil to draw around template. Transfer all alignment markings to fabric. Cut out fabric piece using scissors or rotary cutting equipment.
5. To use an appliqué template, place template on right side of appliqué fabric. Use a mechanical pencil with a very fine lead to lightly draw around template, leaving at least $^1/_2$" between shapes; repeat for number of appliqués specified in project instructions. Cut out shapes a scant $^1/_4$" outside drawn line.

ROTARY CUTTING

Rotary cutting has brought speed and accuracy to quiltmaking by allowing quilters to easily cut strips of fabric and then cut those strips into smaller pieces.

*   Place fabric on work surface with fold closest to you.

*   Cut all strips from the selvage-to-selvage width of the fabric unless otherwise indicated in project instructions.

- Square left edge of fabric using rotary cutter and rulers (**Figs. 1 - 2**).

Fig. 1

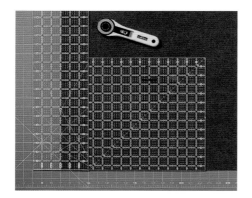

Fig. 2

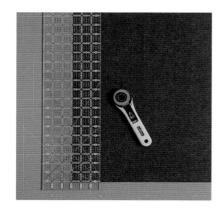

- To cut each strip required for a project, place ruler over cut edge of fabric, aligning desired marking on ruler with cut edge; make cut (**Fig. 3**).

Fig. 3

- When cutting several strips from a single piece of fabric, it is important to make sure that cuts remain at a perfect right angle to the fold; square fabric as needed.

PIECING

Precise cutting, followed by accurate piecing, will ensure that all pieces of quilt top fit together well.

- Set sewing machine stitch length for approximately 11 stitches per inch.

- Use neutral-colored general-purpose sewing thread (not quilting thread) in needle and in bobbin.

- An accurate $1/4$" seam allowance is *essential*. Presser feet that are $1/4$" wide are available for most sewing machines.

- When piecing, always place pieces right sides together and match raw edges; pin if necessary.

- Chain piecing saves time and will usually result in more accurate piecing.

- Trim away points of seam allowances that extend beyond edges of sewn pieces.

SEWING STRIP SETS

When there are several strips to assemble into a strip set, first sew strips together into pairs, then sew pairs together to form strip set. To help avoid distortion, sew seams in opposite directions (**Fig. 4**).

Fig. 4

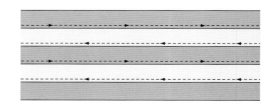

SEWING ACROSS SEAM INTERSECTIONS

When sewing across intersection of two seams, place pieces right sides together and match seams exactly, making sure seam allowances are pressed in opposite directions (**Fig. 5**).

Fig. 5

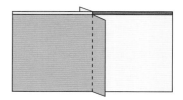

SEWING SHARP POINTS

To ensure sharp points when joining triangular or diagonal pieces, stitch across the center of the "X" (shown in pink) formed on wrong side by previous seams (**Fig. 6**).

Fig. 6

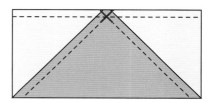

SEWING CURVES

It is important that you mark center of edges on curved pieces, as indicated on patterns. Place pieces right sides together, matching centers (**Fig. 7**). Pin curved edges together at center and corners, clipping as needed (**Fig. 8**). Pin edges together between center and corners, easing in fullness as shown in **Fig. 9**. Sew pieces together along the curved seamline.

Fig. 7

Fig. 8

Fig. 9

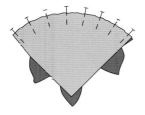

PRESSING

- Use steam iron set on "Cotton" for all pressing.

- Press after sewing each seam.

- Seam allowances are almost always pressed to one side, usually toward darker fabric. However, to reduce bulk it may occasionally be necessary to press seam allowances toward the lighter fabric or even to press them open.

- To prevent dark fabric seam allowance from showing through light fabric, trim darker seam allowance slightly narrower than lighter seam allowance.

- To press long seams, such as those in long strip sets, without curving or other distortion, lay strips across width of the ironing board.

HAND APPLIQUÉ

*In this traditional hand appliqué method, the needle is used to turn the seam allowance under as you sew the appliqué to the background fabric using a Blind Stitch (**page 95, Fig. 40**). When stitching, match the color of thread to the color of appliqué to disguise your stitches. Appliqué each piece starting with the ones directly on the background fabric. It is not necessary to appliqué areas that will be covered by another appliqué. Stitches on the right side of fabric should not show. Clipped areas should be secured with a few extra stitches to prevent fraying.*

1. Place template on right side of appliqué fabric. Use a mechanical pencil with a very fine lead to lightly draw around template, leaving at least $1/2$" between shapes; repeat for number of appliqués specified in project instructions.
2. Cut out shapes a scant $1/4$" outside drawn line. Arrange shapes on background fabric and pin or baste in place.
3. Thread a sharps needle with a single strand of general-purpose sewing thread the color of the appliqué; knot one end.
4. Begin on as straight an edge as possible and use point of needle to turn under a small amount of seam allowance, concealing drawn line on appliqué. Blindstitch appliqué to the background, turning under the seam allowance. Clip inside curves and points up to, but not through, drawn line as you stitch.

BORDERS

Our instructions for cutting borders for bed-size quilts also include an extra 2" at each end for "insurance"; borders will be trimmed after measuring completed center section of quilt top. And, as always, you should match right sides and raw edges and use a 1/4" seam allowance when sewing.

ADDING SQUARED BORDERS

1. Mark the center of each edge of quilt top (**Fig. 10**).

Fig. 10

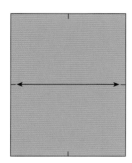

2. Squared borders are usually added to top and bottom, then side edges of the center section of a quilt top. To add top border, measure across center of quilt top to determine length of border (see **Fig. 10**). Trim border to the determined length.
3. Mark center of 1 long edge of border. Matching center marks and raw edges, pin border to quilt top; stitch.
4. Repeat Steps 2 and 3 to add bottom border to quilt top.

5. Measure center of quilt top (including attached borders) to determine length of side borders. Trim borders to the determined measurement. Repeat Step 3 to add side borders to quilt top (**Fig. 11**).

Fig. 11

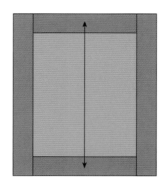

ADDING MITERED BORDERS

1. Mark the center of each edge of quilt top (see **Fig. 10**).
2. Mark center of 1 long edge of top border. Measure across center of quilt top (see **Fig. 10**). Matching center marks and raw edges, pin border to center of quilt top edge. From center of border, measure out 1/2 the width of the quilt top in both directions and mark. Match marks on border with corners of quilt top and pin. Easing in any fullness, pin border to quilt top between center and

corners. Sew border to quilt top, beginning and ending seams exactly 1/4" from each corner of quilt top and backstitching at beginning and end of stitching (**Fig. 12**).

Fig. 12

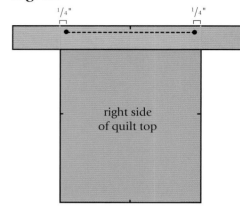

3. Repeat Step 2 to sew bottom, then side borders, to center section of quilt top. To temporarily move first 2 borders out of the way, fold and pin ends as shown in **Fig. 13**.

Fig. 13

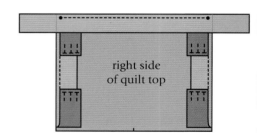

4. Fold 1 corner of quilt top diagonally with right sides together; use rotary cutting ruler to mark stitching line as shown in **Fig. 14**. Pin strips together along drawn line. Sew on drawn line, backstitching at beginning and end of stitching (**Fig. 15**).

Fig. 14

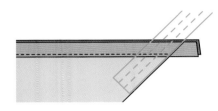

Fig. 15

5. Turn mitered corner right side up. Check to see that there is not a gap at the inner end of the seam and that corner does not pucker.
6. Trim seam allowances to $^1/_4$"; press to 1 side.
7. Repeat Steps 4-6 to miter each remaining corner.

QUILTING

Quilting holds the three layers (top, batting, and backing) of the quilt together and can be done by hand or machine. Because marking, layering, and quilting are interrelated and may be done in different orders depending on circumstances, please read entire **Quilting** *section, pages 89 – 92, before beginning project.*

TYPES OF QUILTING DESIGNS

In the Ditch Quilting
Quilting along seamlines or along edges of appliquéd pieces is called "in the ditch" quilting. This type of quilting should be done on side **opposite** seam allowance and does not have to be marked.

Outline Quilting
Quilting a consistent distance, usually $^1/_4$", from seam or appliqué is called "outline" quilting. Outline quilting may be marked, or $^1/_4$" masking tape may be placed along seamlines for quilting guide. (Do not leave tape on quilt longer than necessary, since it may leave an adhesive residue.)

Motif Quilting
Quilting a design, such as a feathered wreath, is called "motif" quilting. This type of quilting should be marked before basting quilt layers together.

Echo Quilting
Quilting that follows the outline of an appliquéd or pieced design with two or more parallel lines is called "echo" quilting. This type of quilting does not need to be marked.

Channel Quilting
Quilting with straight, parallel lines is called "channel" quilting. This type of quilting may be marked or stitched using a guide.

Crosshatch Quilting
Quilting straight lines in a grid pattern is called "crosshatch" quilting. Lines may be stitched parallel to edges of quilt or stitched diagonally. This type of quilting may be marked or stitched using a guide.

Meandering Quilting
Quilting in random curved lines and swirls is called "meandering" quilting. Quilting lines should not cross or touch each other. This type of quilting does not need to be marked.

Stipple Quilting
Meandering quilting that is very closely spaced is called "stipple" quilting. Stippling will flatten the area quilted and is often stitched in background areas to raise appliquéd or pieced designs. This type of quilting does not need to be marked.

MARKING QUILTING LINES

Quilting lines may be marked using fabric marking pencils, chalk markers, water- or air-soluble pens, or lead pencils.

Simple quilting designs may be marked with chalk or chalk pencil after basting. A small area may be marked, then quilted, before moving to next area to be marked. Intricate designs should be marked before basting using a more durable marker.

Caution: Pressing may permanently set some marks. **Test** different markers **on scrap fabric** to find one that marks clearly and can be thoroughly removed.

A wide variety of pre-cut quilting stencils, as well as entire books of quilting patterns, are available. Using a stencil makes it easier to mark intricate or repetitive designs.

To make a stencil from a pattern, center template plastic over pattern and use a permanent marker to trace pattern onto plastic. Use a craft knife with single or double blade to cut channels along traced lines (**Fig. 16**).

Fig. 16

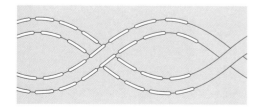

PREPARING THE BACKING

To allow for slight shifting of quilt top during quilting, backing should be approximately 4" larger on all sides. Yardage requirements listed for quilt backings are calculated for 43"/44"w fabric. Using 90"w or 108"w fabric for the backing of a bed-sized quilt may eliminate piecing. To piece a backing using 43"/44"w fabric, use the following instructions.

1. Measure length and width of quilt top; add 8" to each measurement.
2. If determined width is 79" or less, cut backing fabric into two lengths slightly longer than determined *length* measurement. Trim selvages. Place lengths with right sides facing and sew long edges together, forming tube (**Fig. 17**). Match seams and press along one fold (**Fig. 18**). Cut along pressed fold to form single piece (**Fig. 19**).

Fig. 17   **Fig. 18**

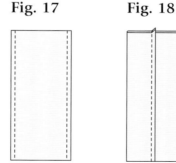

Fig. 19

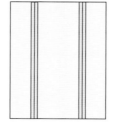

3. If determined width is more than 79", it may require less fabric yardage if the backing is pieced horizontally. Divide determined *length* measurement by 40" to determine how many widths will be needed. Cut required number of widths the determined *width* measurement. Trim selvages. Sew long edges together to form single piece.
4. Trim backing to size determined in Step 1; press seam allowances open.

CHOOSING THE BATTING

The appropriate batting will make quilting easier. For fine hand quilting, choose low-loft batting. All cotton or cotton/polyester blend battings work well for machine quilting because the cotton helps "grip" quilt layers. If quilt is to be tied, a high-loft batting, sometimes called extra-loft or fat batting, may be used to make quilt "fluffy."

Types of batting include cotton, polyester, wool, cotton/polyester blend, cotton/wool blend, and silk.

When selecting batting, refer to package labels for characteristics and care instructions. Cut batting same size as prepared backing.

ASSEMBLING THE QUILT

1. Examine wrong side of quilt top closely; trim any seam allowances and clip any threads that may show through front of the quilt. Press quilt top, being careful not to "set" any marked quilting lines.

2. Place backing *wrong* side up on flat surface. Use masking tape to tape edges of backing to surface. Place batting on top of backing fabric. Smooth batting gently, being careful not to stretch or tear. Center quilt top *right* side up on batting.

3. If hand quilting, begin in center and work toward outer edges to hand baste all layers together. Use long stitches and place basting lines approximately 4" apart (**Fig. 20**). Smooth fullness or wrinkles toward outer edges.

Fig. 20

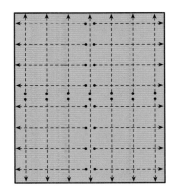

4. If machine quilting, use 1" rustproof safety pins to "pin-baste" all layers together, spacing pins approximately 4" apart. Begin at center and work toward outer edges to secure all layers. If possible, place pins away from areas that will be quilted, although pins may be removed as needed when quilting.

HAND QUILTING

The quilting stitch is a basic running stitch that forms a broken line on quilt top and backing. Stitches on quilt top and backing should be straight and equal in length.

1. Secure center of quilt in hoop or frame. Check quilt top and backing to make sure they are smooth. To help prevent puckers, always begin quilting in the center of quilt and work toward outside edges.

2. Thread needle with 18" – 20" length of quilting thread; knot one end. Using thimble, insert needle into quilt top and batting approximately $1/2$" from quilting line. Bring needle up on quilting line (**Fig. 21**); when knot catches on quilt top, give thread a quick, short pull to "pop" knot through fabric into batting (**Fig. 22**).

Fig. 21

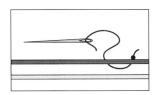

Fig. 22

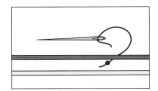

3. Holding needle with sewing hand and placing other hand underneath quilt, use thimble to push tip of needle down through all layers. As soon as needle touches finger underneath, use that finger to push tip of needle only back up through layers to top of quilt. (The amount of needle showing above fabric determines length of quilting stitch.) Referring to **Fig. 23**, rock needle up and down, taking three to six stitches before bringing needle and thread completely through layers. Check back of quilt to make sure stitches are going through all layers. If necessary, make one stitch at a time when quilting through seam allowances or along curves and corners.

Fig. 23

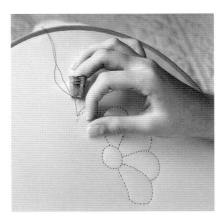

4. At end of thread, knot thread close to fabric and "pop" knot into batting; clip thread close to fabric.

5. Move hoop as often as necessary. Thread may be left dangling and picked up again after returning to that part of quilt.

MACHINE QUILTING METHODS

Use general-purpose thread in bobbin. Do not use quilting thread. Thread the needle of machine with general-purpose thread or transparent monofilament thread to make quilting blend with quilt top fabrics. Use decorative thread, such as a metallic or contrasting-color general-purpose thread, to make quilting lines stand out more.

Straight-Line Quilting

The term "straight-line" is somewhat deceptive, since curves (especially gentle ones) as well as straight lines can be stitched with this technique.

1. Set stitch length for six to ten stitches per inch and attach walking foot to sewing machine.
2. Determine which section of quilt will have longest continuous quilting line, oftentimes the area from center top to center bottom. Roll up and secure each edge of quilt to help reduce the bulk, keeping fabrics smooth. Smaller projects may not need to be rolled.

3. Begin stitching on longest quilting line, using very short stitches for the first 1/4" to "lock" quilting. Stitch across project, using one hand on each side of walking foot to slightly spread fabric and to guide fabric through machine. Lock stitches at end of quilting line.
4. Continue machine quilting, stitching longer quilting lines first to stabilize quilt before moving on to other areas.

Free-Motion Quilting

Free-motion quilting may be free-form or may follow a marked pattern.
1. Attach darning foot to sewing machine and lower or cover feed dogs.
2. Position quilt under darning foot; lower foot. Holding top thread, take a stitch and pull bobbin thread to top of quilt. To "lock" beginning of quilting line, hold top and bobbin threads while making three to five stitches in place.
3. Use one hand on each side of darning foot to slightly spread fabric and to move fabric through the machine. Even stitch length is achieved by using smooth, flowing hand motion and steady machine speed. Slow machine speed and fast hand movement will create long stitches. Fast machine speed and slow hand movement will create short stitches. Move quilt sideways, back and forth, in a circular motion, or in a random motion to create desired designs; do not rotate quilt. Lock stitches at end of each quilting line.

MAKING A HANGING SLEEVE

Attaching a hanging sleeve to back of wall hanging or quilt before the binding is added allows project to be displayed on wall.
1. Measure width of quilt top edge and subtract 1". Cut piece of fabric 7"w by determined measurement.
2. Press short edges of fabric piece 1/4" to wrong side; press edges 1/4" to wrong side again and machine stitch in place.
3. Matching wrong sides, fold piece in half lengthwise to form tube.
4. Follow project instructions to sew binding to quilt top and to trim backing and batting. Before Blindstitching binding to backing, match raw edges and stitch hanging sleeve to center top edge on back of quilt.
5. Finish binding quilt, treating hanging sleeve as part of backing.
6. Blindstitch bottom of hanging sleeve to backing, taking care not to stitch through to front of quilt.
7. Insert dowel or slat into hanging sleeve.

BINDING

Binding encloses the raw edges of quilt. Because of its stretchiness, bias binding works well for binding projects with curves or rounded corners and tends to lie smooth and flat in any given circumstance. Binding may also be cut from straight lengthwise or crosswise grain of fabric.

MAKING CONTINUOUS BIAS STRIP BINDING

Bias strips for binding can simply be cut and pieced to desired length. However, when a long length of binding is needed, the "continuous" method is quick and accurate.

1. Cut square from binding fabric the size indicated in project instructions. Cut square in half diagonally to make two triangles.
2. With right sides together and using ¹/₄" seam allowance, sew triangles together (**Fig. 24**); press seam allowances open.

Fig. 24

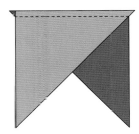

3. On wrong side of fabric, draw lines the width of binding as specified in project instructions (**Fig. 25**). Cut off any remaining fabric less than this width.

Fig. 25

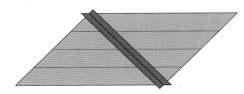

4. With right sides inside, bring short edges together to form tube; match raw edges so that first drawn line of top section meets second drawn line of bottom section (**Fig. 26**).

Fig. 26

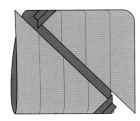

5. Carefully pin edges together by inserting pins through drawn lines at point where drawn lines intersect, making sure pins go through intersections on both sides. Using ¹/₄" seam allowance, sew edges together; press seam allowances open.

6. To cut continuous strip, begin cutting along first drawn line (**Fig. 27**). Continue cutting along drawn line around tube.

Fig. 27

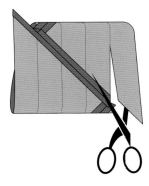

7. Trim ends of bias strip square.
8. Matching wrong sides and raw edges, carefully press bias strip in half lengthwise to complete binding.

ATTACHING BINDING WITH MITERED CORNERS

1. Beginning with one end near center on bottom edge of quilt, lay binding around quilt to make sure that seams in binding will not end up at a corner. Adjust placement if necessary. Matching raw edges of binding to raw edge of quilt top, pin binding to right side of quilt along one edge.
2. When you reach first corner, mark ¹/₄" from corner of quilt top (**Fig. 28**).

Fig. 28

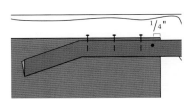

3. Beginning approximately 10" from end of binding and using $1/4$" seam allowance, sew binding to quilt, backstitching at beginning of stitching and at mark (**Fig. 29**). Lift needle out of fabric and clip thread.

Fig. 29

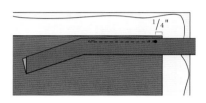

4. Fold binding as shown in **Figs. 30 – 31** and pin binding to adjacent side, matching raw edges. When you've reached the next corner, mark $1/4$" from edge of quilt top.

Fig. 30

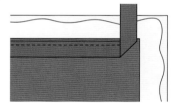

Fig. 31

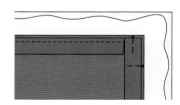

5. Backstitching at edge of quilt top, sew pinned binding to quilt (**Fig. 32**); backstitch at the next mark. Lift needle out of fabric and clip thread.

Fig. 32

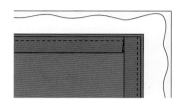

6. Continue sewing binding to quilt, stopping approximately 10" from starting point (**Fig. 33**).

Fig. 33

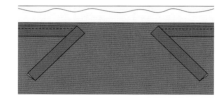

7. Bring beginning and end of binding to center of opening and fold each end back, leaving a $1/4$" space between folds (**Fig. 34**). Finger press folds.

Fig. 34

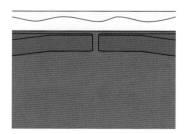

8. Unfold ends of binding and draw a line across wrong side in finger-pressed crease. Draw a line through the lengthwise pressed fold of binding at the same spot to create a cross mark. With edge of ruler at cross mark, line up 45° angle marking on ruler with one long side of binding. Draw a diagonal line from edge to edge. Repeat on remaining end, making sure that the two diagonal lines are angled the same way (**Fig. 35**).

Fig. 35

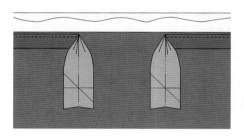

9. Matching right sides and diagonal lines, pin binding ends together at right angles (**Fig. 36**).

Fig. 36

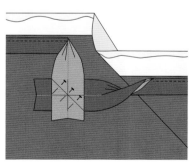

10. Machine stitch along diagonal line (**Fig. 37**), removing pins as you stitch.

Fig. 37

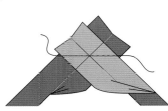

11. Lay binding against quilt to double check that it is correct length.
12. Trim binding ends, leaving $1/4$" seam allowance; press seam open. Stitch binding to quilt.
13. Trim backing and batting a scant $1/4$" larger than quilt top so that batting and backing will fill the binding when it is folded over to quilt backing.
14. On one edge of quilt, fold binding over to quilt backing and pin pressed edge in place, covering stitching line (**Fig. 38**). On adjacent side, fold binding over, forming a mitered corner (**Fig. 39**). Repeat to pin remainder of binding in place.

Fig. 38   **Fig. 39**

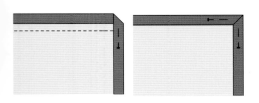

15. Blindstitch binding to backing, taking care not to stitch through to front of quilt. To blindstitch, come up at 1, go down at 2, and come up at 3 (**Fig. 40**). Length of stitches may be varied as desired.

Fig. 40

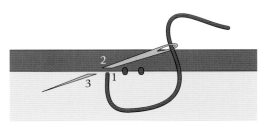

ATTACHING BINDING WITH OVERLAPPED CORNERS

1. Matching raw edges and using $1/4$" seam allowance, sew a length of binding to top and bottom edges on right side of quilt.
2. Trim backing and batting from top and bottom edges a scant $1/4$" larger than quilt top so that batting and backing will fill the binding when it is folded over to quilt backing.
3. Trim ends of top and bottom binding even with edges of quilt top. Fold binding over to quilt backing and pin pressed edges in place, covering stitching line (**Fig. 41**); blindstitch binding to backing.

Fig. 41

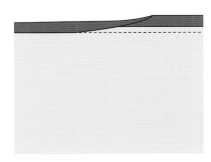

4. Leaving approximately 1¹/₂" of binding at each end, stitch a length of binding to each side edge of quilt. Trim backing and batting as in Step 2.

5. Trim each end of binding ¹/₂" longer than bound edge. Fold each end of binding over to quilt backing (**Fig. 42**); pin in place. Fold binding over to quilt backing and blindstitch in place, taking care not to stitch through to front of quilt.

Fig. 42

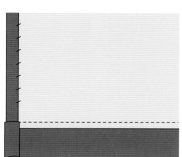

SIGNING AND DATING YOUR QUILT

A completed quilt is a work of art and should be signed and dated. There are many different ways to do this and numerous books on the subject. The label should reflect the style of the quilt, the occasion or person for which it was made, and the quilter's own particular talents. Following are suggestions for recording the history of quilt or adding a sentiment for future generations.

- Embroider quilter's name, date, and any additional information on quilt top or backing. Matching floss, such as cream floss on white border, will leave a subtle record. Bright or contrasting floss will make the information stand out.

- Make label from muslin and use permanent marker to write information. Use different colored permanent markers to make label more decorative. Stitch label to back of quilt.

- Use photo-transfer paper to add image to white or cream fabric label. Stitch label to back of quilt.

- Piece an extra block from quilt top pattern to use as label. Add information with permanent fabric pen. Appliqué block to back of quilt.

Metric Conversion Chart			
Inches x 2.54 = centimeters (cm)		Yards x .9144 = meters (m)	
Inches x 25.4 = millimeters (mm)		Yards x 91.44 = centimeters (cm)	
Inches x .0254 = meters (m)		Centimeters x .3937 = inches (")	
		Meters x 1.0936 = yards (yd)	

Standard Equivalents					
¹/₈"	3.2 mm	0.32 cm	¹/₈ yard	11.43 cm	0.11 m
¹/₄"	6.35 mm	0.635 cm	¹/₄ yard	22.86 cm	0.23 m
³/₈"	9.5 mm	0.95 cm	³/₈ yard	34.29 cm	0.34 m
¹/₂"	12.7 mm	1.27 cm	¹/₂ yard	45.72 cm	0.46 m
⁵/₈"	15.9 mm	1.59 cm	⁵/₈ yard	57.15 cm	0.57 m
³/₄"	19.1 mm	1.91 cm	³/₄ yard	68.58 cm	0.69 m
⁷/₈"	22.2 mm	2.22 cm	⁷/₈ yard	80 cm	0.8 m
1 "	25.4 mm	2.54 cm	1 yard	91.44 cm	0.91 m